PLAY IT AWAY

A WORKAHOLIC'S CURE FOR ANXIETY

CHARLIE HOEHN

ISBN: 978-0-615-91817-4

TABLE OF CONTENTS

1

MY ANXIETY STORY

For a long time, I thought I was going crazy. I'd convinced myself that something horribly wrong was about to happen. I thought I would be attacked or arrested every time I left my apartment.

I saw criminals and undercover cops everywhere I went. I was sure that there was an impending disaster that would melt the social contract and pit my neighbors against me. All that "world is coming to an end" talk? I believed it. And the only thing that made me feel safe was worrying.

Every moment was exhausting. I dreaded being around more than one person at a time. I eyed everyone like they were judging me, pitying me, or trying to manipulate me. My attention was constantly divided. One half of me pretended to be normal while the other half tried to keep it together. I could feel parts of my face twitching, like I was about to crack. My hands shook constantly. It got so bad that I couldn't drink a glass of water without spilling.

I tried to behave like nothing was wrong, when all I wanted was to lock myself in a room and curl up in a ball. I felt fragile, weak, and hollow. If someone had tapped me on the chest, my body would have shattered.

I didn't want to be around anyone – not because I stopped liking people; I just didn't want them to catch my weird energy. Everything felt forced and fake and exhausting. If someone experienced something great, I didn't care. If someone went through something horrible, I didn't care. If a friend wanted to go to the movies, I'd say, "Yeah, let's do that," but felt like they were trying to drain the little bit of life I had left.

I didn't have thoughts of *I want to kill myself*, but I did think *I want this to be done*. There was no meaning, purpose, joy, excitement, stimulation, or sex drive. I wearily watched my girlfriend cry after I confided that I felt dead inside, all the time, and didn't know how to fix it.

I was ashamed, because I couldn't explain it without feeling like a failure. How could I possibly be so miserable and unhappy? What right did I have to feel this way? Couldn't I just tough it out?

I laid on the ground in the fetal position for 20 minutes one night, wondering whether I should call an ambulance. My heart was beating so hard and fast that I could actually hear it, and my left hand was going numb. It was my first panic attack. I closed my eyes and trembled as two deafening thoughts played on loop in my mind:

You are going crazy.

You are going to die.

There's no 'I' in anxiety. Wait. Yes there is.
Oh my god oh my god oh my god.

— ELIZA BAYNE

My anxiety lasted for more than a year. It affected how I breathed, how I thought, how I ate, how I slept, and how I talked. I was serious and tired and afraid, all the time. I wanted so badly to return to my normal, lively, carefree self. But I had no idea how to shake it.

I scheduled an appointment with my doctor. I told her about the panic attacks, and explained the inner turmoil I was battling. She suggested that I get an EKG at the hospital, just to make sure my heart was okay. Then she gave me a prescription for a pill she described as "a non-addictive version of Xanax."

She said it would help me sleep, and that I'd feel better in a few days.

I couldn't believe it. I practically skipped home, clutching the little orange bottle to my chest. I finally had an escape hatch from my relentless tension and fear.

Just as I was about to take one of the pills, I decided to look up the brand on Wikipedia. My heart sunk as I read the warnings listed on the page:

High addictive potential...

Withdrawal symptoms can range from anxiety and insomnia to seizures and psychosis...

Great. Instead of suffering from anxiety, I can become a psychotic-epileptic-insomniac junkie...who *still* suffers from anxiety.

I read through dozens of blog posts and forum discussions about the drug. Nearly everyone said it stopped working after the first week. I couldn't find a single testimonial of this pill curing anyone's anxiety.

I took the little orange bottle to my bathroom and reluctantly flushed all 30 pills down the toilet.

I was extremely discouraged, but my desperation to cure myself was stronger than ever. I spent the next several months trying to conquer my inner demons. I researched and tried *everything…*

- ✓ Meditation
- ✓ Deep breathing exercises
- ✓ Yoga
- ✓ Journaling
- ✓ Therapy
- ✓ Therapy books
- ✓ Aromatherapy
- ✓ Acupuncture
- ✓ Massages
- ✓ Floatation tanks
- ✓ Chiropractors
- ✓ Naturopaths
- ✓ Spiritual healers
- ✓ Volunteering
- ✓ High-intensity workouts
- ✓ Long runs
- ✓ Super clean diets
- ✓ Supplements
- ✓ Psychedelics
- ✓ Extended fasting
- ✓ Prayer

I even took a six-week course made specifically for men who wanted to overcome anxiety.

A few of these things helped, but most of them didn't. Some of them made things worse.

Then one day, it happened. I discovered the cure for my anxiety. It took me a moment to fully comprehend it, but when my mind processed that I'd found the solution, I started laughing. The answer had been so obvious all along.

In less than one month, I was back to my old self. I woke up one day and nearly overlooked how great I felt. My anxiety subsided so steadily that I no longer noticed it. Just like that, it was gone. I was free.

The process for healing myself was fun, painless, and immediately effective. I have no fear that those awful feelings will ever return. If they do, I'll be able to wipe them out right away.[1]

---

[1] If you'd like to watch a quick video summary of my cure and the contents of this book, visit playitaway.me/video.

2

WHY I WROTE THIS BOOK

In May of 2013, I wrote a lengthy essay called *How I Cured My Anxiety* and published it on my blog, CharlieHoehn.com. I didn't have a huge audience, but I suspected the message would strike a chord with my readers. It did.

Within two weeks, the post was read and shared by tens of thousands of people. I received hundreds of messages from anxiety sufferers all over the world. The post was so popular that it shot up to the #1 position on Google for the search phrase "cure anxiety" – right above Oprah.com.

My post was honest, but it was incomplete. It didn't contain everything that helped me; only my first major breakthrough. I wanted to share all of the techniques that put my life back on track and healed my pain. That's the book you're reading right now.

I wrote *Play It Away* because I couldn't find anything like it when I was searching for my cure. That's the point of this book: to create for other people what I wished had existed. I was so jaded after trying all these different things that never seemed to help. Then a few key pieces clicked into place, and I was back to normal. And at the risk of sounding like a late-night infomercial, the cure for my anxiety was so much easier than I imagined.

It's my sincerest hope that, by sharing my entire story, you too will find your way back to health and happiness. But before we continue, I need to lay down a quick disclaimer. Just so there's no confusion, please understand:

I am not a health care professional, and while a lot of these chapters contain actionable advice that you can use in your life, **this book is about MY experiences curing MY anxiety**. What I did might work for you, or it might not. You need to figure that out for yourself by using your own judgment, not just by blindly following my advice (or anyone's advice, really).[2]

In order to properly treat anxiety, one must identify and fix what is causing it. The primary source of my anxiety was me. I was the creator of my own suffering. I just couldn't see it.

---

[2] The methods I used to heal my anxiety are backed up by a lot of data and scientific research. I won't weigh you down with those details in the text because that's not what this book is about. However, if you want to double-check the validity of any of my techniques, just visit playitaway.me/endnotes.

3

MY WORKAHOLIC STORY

If you work for a living,

why do you kill yourself working?

— THE GOOD, THE BAD, AND THE UGLY

My brain felt swollen, like it was pushing against my skull. I looked down at my iPhone. Good lord. 60 hours straight. Wide awake, no sleep, for 60 hours straight. Yet I was still lively and sharp, thanks to the magic pill.

For four days, I'd supercharged my energy with a powerful nootropic; a brain drug typically reserved for fighter pilots and narcoleptics. If you've seen the movie *Limitless*, well, that pill actually exists. The drug's primary function is to silence the body's pleas for sleep. Lucky for me. Rest was a luxury I couldn't afford.

I'd secretly taken this brain drug, without my boss knowing, so I could be great at my job. I was in charge of coordinating the *Opening the Kimono* event — a private conference on next-generation content marketing, hosted by Tim Ferriss.

Most people knew Tim as the author of two mega-bestselling books: *The 4-Hour Workweek* and *The 4-Hour Body*. The driving themes of Tim's work were effectiveness and efficiency — getting better results, in less time, with less effort. In *The 4HWW*, Tim gave readers step-by-step blueprints for creating online businesses, generating passive income, outsourcing work, and taking mini-retirements. In *The 4HB*, Tim revealed how to lose 20 pounds of fat in one month (without exercise), how to triple fat loss with cold exposure, and how to produce 15-minute female orgasms. Both books sold more than a million copies each, and Tim was a star in the publishing world.

In addition to being a bestselling author, Tim was also a successful angel investor and advisor (his portfolio included Facebook, Twitter, Uber, Evernote, and many others). He was also — and I'm not exaggerating — a Chinese kickboxing champion, a horseback archer, a world record holder in tango, and a polyglot (fluent in five languages). The man was the embodiment of achievement, and I was lucky enough to have him as my mentor.

I'd been working with Tim for nearly three years as his Director of Special Projects. It was a dream job I'd worked hard to land, and I'd reaped countless benefits. In the time we'd known each other, he'd personally introduced me to his entire network of successful friends, given me a world-class education in entrepreneurship, and helped build my portfolio into an expansive showcase of incredible work.

I was 25 years old at the time, living in Russian Hill in San Francisco. Each morning, I'd walk over to my neighborhood café, sit down with my laptop, and work until nightfall on my weekly tasks. Whenever I finished a given job, I'd ask Tim for more work. Things multiplied quickly, and I soon had a plethora of responsibilities: assistant, researcher, editor, marketer, videographer, photographer, customer service, project manager... And now, I was his conference coordinator. *Opening The Kimono* was my biggest challenge to date.

More than 130 authors and entrepreneurs, from all over the world, paid $10,000 apiece for admission to Tim's conference. And while I was confident we would successfully make it through this four-day event, I was also completely overwhelmed by the complexity of the task. There were so many moving parts.

I was terrified of screwing up. If something went wrong, I

would need to fix it with superhuman speed. Somehow, I had to stay awake for the entire event...

And so, in my desperation, I visited an overseas pharmaceutical website, where I ordered the most powerful brain drug on the market.

The pills arrived just before the event. I took one every morning. Each day, I expected to pass out randomly from exhaustion. But it never happened; I stayed alert and wide-awake the whole time. The pills really, really worked. During the course of the four-day seminar, I slept a grand total of *six hours*. And just as I'd hoped, I was great at my job.

The event was a whirlwind, but we managed to pull it off. On the final day, everyone gave us a standing ovation. Attendees ran up to hug us and said it was the best conference they'd ever been to. Our inboxes were filled with dozens of glowing reviews and thank you notes.

WITH TIM FERRISS

I was in shock. After months of working around the clock, we'd exceeded all expectations, including our own. Tim gave me a hearty congratulations, and said he was amazed how well we'd done.

I was proud, happy, and very tired when I arrived back home. But later that night, my body started sending out emergency signals, warning me that something horribly wrong was happening.

My heart was racing. My vision was blurred. I had a pounding headache that wouldn't stop. Sounds drifted sluggishly into my ears, and I could barely stand upright.

For the first time in my life, I felt completely and utterly burned out.

—⟋⟍—

A few days later, I went back to work. We were just getting started on our next big project: *The 4-Hour Chef*.

Two years prior, I helped Tim edit and launch his second book, *The 4-Hour Body*. I was immensely proud to have played a part in the book's success; it was the pinnacle of my career. On the other hand, *The 4-Hour Body* had been the most stressful undertaking of my life. Tim and I half-joked that the book nearly killed us. I was very hesitant to jump in for round two.

Tim offered to double my salary if I helped him complete *The 4-Hour Chef*. It was a generous offer, and I was immediately interested in taking it. I'd be making more money than I'd know what to do with, and I'd have another cool achievement under my belt. What did I have to lose? After a moment's pause, we shook on it.

I felt incredibly fortunate to be in that position, especially since so many people I knew were either unemployed or working in jobs they hated. My family and friends all congratulated me. From a distance, things looked great.

But on the inside, I was flailing. I'd completely lost balance, and I couldn't even recognize that I was destroying myself.

You see, I liked to think of myself as busy and important, so I was tethered to the internet seven days a week. I communicated with people primarily through screens. I spent all day long sitting indoors. I drank coffee all week, and drank alcohol all weekend. I only stopped working when I was sleeping. And then I stopped sleeping.

I just couldn't stop myself from working all the time. It didn't matter what else was going on in my life; work was everything. No one seemed to mind, because practically everyone around me behaved the same way. All of my friends and colleagues were workaholics. Several buddies of mine were pulling 16-hour workdays. My friend in medical school was popping Adderall like it was candy. All of us were destroying ourselves during the week, and punishing our livers on the weekend. We didn't take vacations. We didn't take breaks. Work was life.

Here's the thing: I was a workaholic long before I met Tim. I'd always stayed up late. I'd always spent hours at a time staring at screens. The difference now was that my state of mind had changed. I took my work very seriously. And because my entire life revolved around work, life stopped being fun.

Each week, I felt increasingly sick, exhausted, and apathetic. My eyes sunk back and grew dark circles beneath them. My forehead developed thick stress lines. My hands started shaking. I felt like I was always on the verge of crying. I didn't understand what was wrong with me, so I just tried to work my way through it.

Then the deadline for *The 4-Hour Chef* got pushed back three months.

Then a family member died.

Then my close friend attempted suicide.

When Tim and I met up for dinner the following week, I told him very meekly:

"I can't do this anymore. I have to quit."

Tim didn't argue with me. He understood where I was coming from, and offered his support in whatever I was going to do next. It was a relief to part on amicable terms, but I felt weaker than ever. I was already feeling the pressure to get back to work, but what would I do? My identity was gone. I decided to take a couple weeks off. Then another week... And another...

I spent the next two months being unemployed and feeling awful. Every day, I'd go through the motions of my old work routine without actually doing anything. I compulsively checked email all day long, stayed up until 4:00AM, and slept a few hours each night. I received a handful of job offers and turned them all down, recoiling at the thought of having to go back to work.

The worst part was the guilt. I felt enormously guilty every second I wasn't doing something that could advance my career or earn money. I would pace around like a neurotic rat, coming up with random chores to distract myself. When the chores were finished, I'd think, "Okay... Now what?" Any activity that didn't feel productive – sleeping in, watching TV, taking a trip – filled me with regret. There was this gnawing sense that I was wasting time. I was losing money. And yet, I had no desire to work.

I started wondering if I'd screwed up my life very badly. *Hadn't I been living The Dream? Did I just throw away everything I'd worked for?* I started feeling very anxious. I wanted to do something big, to reinvent my career, to make a name for myself so I could be successful. What that something would be, I didn't know.

Then one day, two of my friends, Chad Mureta (whom I'd met at the *Kimono* event) and Jason Adams, suggested that we start a mobile app company together. They were both sharp entrepreneurs and savvy marketers, and Chad was already making millions from the apps he'd developed.

INTERVIEWING CHAD MURETA

Finally, I thought, *here's a job that makes sense.* I could be one of the founders of a cool tech startup, working on fun projects with my smart friends, in one of the most exciting industries on the planet. The Draw Something app had recently been acquired for $250 million, then Facebook acquired Instagram for $1 billion. I thought, *This gig might make me a millionaire by the end of the year! This is it...*

I was so relieved to feel productive again. I strolled into the office each day to work on my laptop until late in the evening. I sat down, stared at my computer screen for several hours, and drank coffee. When I got home, I worked on my laptop until 4:00AM, slept for a few hours, then started all over again.

We spent the first month putting together an online course called *App Empire*, which walked people through the entire process of starting their own app business. It required many sleepless nights to get it finished on time, but we managed to pull it off.

The launch of the course was a success, raking in $2 million dollars in revenue over the course of 10 days.[3] We spent the next two months doing weekly webinars, walking customers through each lesson and answering their questions. In our spare time, we worked on our app ideas.

At some point in the third month, I realized: *I didn't care about apps*. I knew how to make them, and I knew how to succeed in the app market, but I just didn't care. I didn't really use apps and I never got excited about them.

---

[3] If you said "WTF!" after reading that sentence, I don't blame you. But our results were somewhat typical in the high-cost information product world. When you combine a $2,000 course with a huge list of potential customers (and three guys who know a lot about online marketing), you get a multi-million dollar product launch.

I asked myself, *Why am I really doing this work?* Well, the job gave me an excuse to hang out with my friends during the day, rather than being holed up alone in my apartment. But that was only a small part of it. The honest answer was:

Status. Money. Guilt.

I wanted to impress other people with my "success" of founding a company. I wanted to be rich. And I wanted to avoid feeling bad for not working.

The problem was... I didn't really care about what I was doing. There was this weird disconnect, like apps should have been the natural progression in my career. But it just never felt right. It felt forced.

I quit my job that week.

Once again, I experienced "success" and walked away from it. Only this time, I was riddled with anxiety.

I started to think I was going to be punished for not being productive, for not making money, for not having my life figured out. I didn't know how or when, but I was certain it was going to happen. Everything was coming to a head. It was only a matter of time before something really bad happened...

I was in a bad place for a long time after I quit those jobs. I didn't have a life or identity outside of my career, so I had nothing to fall back on. I was too scared and proud to reach out to anyone for help, so I bottled my feelings up and stumbled around for the next year. It was the worst I've ever felt in my life.

It'd be very easy for me to manufacture a villain in this story. I could tell you that I was pushed too hard, or that no one cared about how I felt. But that's not the truth. I was the one who chose to stay up until 4:00AM. I was the one pouring caffeine down my throat every hour. I was the one who secretly ordered brain pills. I was the one who isolated myself from friends and kept my feelings hidden. Everything I did that fueled my anxiety was my choice.

The truth is that all of my emotional issues would have unfolded for me at some point in my life, regardless of whom I was working with. I was the creator of my own anxiety, and I was the one who broke myself with my workaholic habits. I just didn't recognize how destructive my behavior was because I thought it was normal.

I wish someone had held up a mirror to show me I was the

problem, but that never happened. No one knew the full extent of my situation but me, and I was in denial. It's worth taking a moment to ask yourself:

- ✓ Do I feel guilty or anxious when I'm not working?
- ✓ Have I stopped playing with my friends?
- ✓ Do all of my daily activities revolve around building a more successful career?
- ✓ Am I sleeping fewer than eight hours per night?
- ✓ Am I consuming stimulants multiple times per day to hide my exhaustion?
- ✓ Am I sitting still and staring at screens for most of my waking hours?
- ✓ Do I interact with people primarily through screens?
- ✓ Am I indoors all day long, depriving myself of fresh air and sunlight?
- ✓ Do I depend on alcohol or drugs to cope with social situations outside of work?

If you said 'Yes' to most of those questions, then you are reading the right book. When I was at my worst, I was doing all of these things on a daily basis. I was fueling my own anxiety and I couldn't even see it.

My perceived lack of productivity, lack of money, and the unknown future kept me in a constant state of panic. Every day was a haze of fear and exhaustion. For more than a year, I tried everything to pull myself out of this state of living death. Nothing seemed to help, and I nearly lost hope.

Then one night, I had my first major breakthrough, which laid the foundation to cure my anxiety. This breakthrough happened in a flash. The emotional burden of non-stop worry was lifted, and I could finally breathe again.

It wasn't hard. It didn't cost me anything. It was only a choice.

4

HOW I CURED MY ANXIETY

Some people have been on the ride for a long time,
and they begin to question, "Is this real, or is this
just a ride?" And other people have remembered,
and they come back to us and they say, "Hey,
don't worry; don't be afraid, ever, because
this is just a ride."

— BILL HICKS

One night, while I was looking at a friend's book collection, I stumbled upon an interesting title — *Play: How it Shapes the Brain, Opens the Imagination, and Invigorates the Soul,* by Dr. Stuart Brown. I sat down and read the book in one sitting.

The message of *Play* hit me like a brick wall. I could finally see how I was creating my own suffering:

I was constantly depriving myself of play!

The problem was *my state of mind*. For years, I'd mentally blocked myself from having guilt-free fun. I was a workaholic who was extremely adept at rejecting everything that wasn't productive. I couldn't enjoy any form of leisure if it didn't earn money or help my career.

CHECKING EMAIL AT 2:00AM, IN BUENOS AIRES

I didn't allow myself to play because that meant I wasn't working. But I couldn't really work because I always felt tired and jaded. Even after I finished working for the day, I'd still check my email a dozen times between midnight and 2:00AM. I knew it was dumb and "What could be so important?" and "You need your sleep," but I did it anyway. I had to stay connected to my work. I was oblivious to the fact that my nerves were being frayed every waking hour, and that I desperately needed fun face-to-face time with real human beings.

What made matters worse were my unhealthy routines:

✓ Sitting and staring at screens for 12 hours a day
✓ Pounding coffee and energy drinks every hour

✓ Binge drinking with friends on the weekend

My weeks were a cycle of mental over-stimulation, physical inactivity, social isolation, and emotional numbing. I didn't get outside. I didn't move. I didn't sleep. I didn't play with my friends. I just kept working.

Even when I was technically "playing" with my friends, I always felt guilty. My mind was elsewhere: what I did wrong in the past, how I was compromising my future, and how I was wasting the present. I was incapable of *being in the moment*. I had to get back to work.

What would the world do without me and my important work?

Without realizing it, I became very serious and intense, even though I'd never been that way in my entire life. I approached everything with this *Life Is Serious* mentality...

Work	=	Slavery
Exercise	=	Chore
Food	=	Guilt
Friendship	=	Obligation
Love	=	Social construct

Somehow, I managed to suck the joy out of every single

aspect of my existence. I was so intensely critical of life that I blocked my ability to enjoy it.

I was convinced that the real world was a miserable grind for adults, and that I needed to work even harder if I wanted to enjoy life. Someday, I'd be rich and permanently successful. And when I reached that point, I would allow myself to stop worrying and be happy.

A lack of play should be treated like malnutrition:
it's a health risk to your body and mind.

— STUART BROWN

Have you ever witnessed a little kid working out on a treadmill?

Or meeting up with a friend to chat over coffee?

Or attending a networking conference to hand out business cards?

Hell no! That stuff is LAME and BORING. If you saw a kid doing any of those things, you would laugh and wonder what was wrong with them.

Kids don't run to get in shape; they run to feel the wind in their face and the grass beneath their feet.

Kids don't chat over coffee; they make jokes and play games with their friends.

Kids don't network; they bond while they're having fun together.

There is no ego. There is no guilt. There is no past to regret, and no future to worry about. *They just play.*

And that's what I'd forgotten, what I'd been missing, all along.

— ∿ —

The week I decided to start playing again, a friend introduced me to his buddy David via email. David replied with the usual request, asking if I wanted to grab coffee. I paused for a moment, then wrote back:

> Hey David, it's nice to meet you. This is an irregular request, but do you want to play catch at a park? I haven't done that in awhile and it's a lot more stimulating than sitting around and drinking coffee.

His response:

SURE THING. Playing catch sounds like a f*ing blast! I'll ping you in a bit and if we can't do it today, let's play ball tomorrow!

And it was a blast. Playing catch removed the pressure that's so common in business meetings, where both sides are subtly trying to impress each other. Instead of putting ourselves through the usual nonsense, we got to enjoy our game on a warm summer day in the park.

I felt rejuvenated after my first play meeting. I gained a surplus of happiness, which spilled into the rest of my day. Suddenly, I found myself teasing bored cashiers, being more flirtatious, and cracking inappropriate jokes. Just a couple hours of *guilt-free* play reduced my anxiety and increased my confidence.

I had a date scheduled the following night. Rather than trying to be *on* for hours at a time, I decided to think of the night as a series of spontaneous games.

It worked. Our energy was never uptight because we played around the entire time. We ordered whisky Shirley Temples, shot cherry stems through our straws at random people, and cracked jokes about the karaoke singers. There were no attempts to be cool or charming, or thoughts about where the date might take us. It was all about finding ways to make the moment fun.

That was how I wanted all of my meetups to be from that point forward. I just had to ask myself, *What games can we play together?*

My friend Tucker and I started playing home run derby every Saturday. We'd drive over to a high school baseball field with a bucket of balls, a few bats, and our gloves. One of us pitched from behind an L-screen (the net that protects the pitcher from line drives) while the other person hit. We acted like little kids; whooping and hollering each time we hit a home run and talking trash about who was the best hitter.

I wanted to surround myself with more fun people who cracked me up and treated life as a game. If I was always around friends who wanted to play, I knew my anxiety would fade away.

That's when I signed up for something I'd always been too scared to do: improv comedy classes.

For three hours each week, I thrust myself into situations where I was guaranteed to look foolish. At first, I was really nervous and slightly mortified. My heart beat rapidly and my voice quivered whenever I performed in front of 15 other people. But by the end of the first month, improv was a tremendous source of strength for me. And it was the most fun I'd had in years.

All of us were there to *play*, to go with the flow and say "Yes!" to every ridiculous scenario we were thrown into. We all looked like idiots, but after a few classes, none of us cared. The voices in our heads that constantly judged and graded us for not being perfect were silenced. We became desensitized to our fear of failing because *we all screwed up, all the time*. And it didn't matter. We just leaned in, adapted on the fly, and treated every mistake like it was intentional and perfect.

I still remember my first great scene. I crawled out to center stage on my stomach, acting like a prisoner who was about to make a break for his freedom. My partner was supposed to mirror all of my movements, so she crawled out beside me. When we looked at each other in surprise, we launched into an argument about who would escape first. We couldn't yell at each other (we didn't want to get caught), so we just aggressively whispered the whole time. The longer we argued and delayed our escape, the funnier the scene became. Our classmates cracked up as the tension mounted, and our teacher finally ended the scene by saying, "I could watch this all day."

Every improv class reminded me of the father-son baseball

games from Little League. All the kids looked forward to that one game each season because, for a few glorious hours, there were no critics or coaches. Everyone was there to participate and have fun. If someone made an error, no one yelled because we were too busy laughing. The outcome didn't matter. It was true play.

Improv wasn't about keeping score, or self-improvement, or even acting funny. It was about being in the moment and *letting go*. And for a few glorious hours, I didn't need to be my anxious, workaholic, perfectionist self. I could just play around and have guilt-free fun.

And that was how I approached life before anxiety. I never used to worry too much about being successful or surviving in the real world. I just embraced the moment, knowing it was another opportunity to have fun with my friends. Life was a game, and I always allowed myself to play. I wanted it to be that way again.

Then I realized... it could be. In fact, it always had been.

It took me a long time to see it, but I finally realized: I really don't function well when I approach life as *Work*. I have to think of life as *Play*. Otherwise I take everything way too seriously, my health and happiness plummet, and the work I produce is awful.

When I tackle my work with a sense of play — voluntarily, because I'm inherently attracted to it — my creativity and optimism soar. I fall in love with the process. My playful energy becomes contagious, and I'm able to create unique art with the people around me.

All of the fun gigs I landed after college came about because I approached my work through the lens of *Play*. I found interesting projects being run by cool people, and came up with ways to make their customers happier. Then I offered to help them out on a trial basis, for free.

Free work was my license to do fun stuff that mattered to me. And to my surprise, my free work almost always resulted in paid offers.[4] I'd get bonuses and promotions for "going the extra mile." In reality, I wasn't trying to go the extra mile; I was just creating my own fun. For me, coming up with ways to delight the customer was *play*.

Then somewhere along the way, I stopped listening to my inner voice — the one that wanted to have fun. I stopped thinkingof my work as a game; it was simply *Work*. Every day

---

[4] I wrote a short guide called *Recession-Proof Graduate* that details how I did this. You can download it for free at charliehoehn.com/freework.

was serious business. I needed to get more results. I needed to earn more money. I needed to have more success. I needed *more...*

And I missed the point the whole way along.

Now, my state of mind is different. I allow myself to have guilt-free fun in everything I do. My work is a game, and my life is a ride. And you know what? I feel 100 times better than I ever thought I would. I'm back to my normal self. I love life again. And I have no fear that those awful feelings will ever return, because I know the antidote.

Play is the creator of joy. It's the source of fun and love, where our subconscious naturally guides us. Play is the state where we are truly ourselves, once we let go of our egos and fear of looking stupid. It's what facilitates our best friendships, our most treasured memories, and ultimately, our enjoyment of life.

And when it comes to work, play is what's driven and shaped every treasured contribution in the history of mankind:

- ✓ Music
- ✓ Art
- ✓ Books
- ✓ Storytelling
- ✓ Film
- ✓ Comedy

- ✓ Sports
- ✓ Festivals
- ✓ Concerts
- ✓ Holidays
- ✓ Dance
- ✓ Cooking
- ✓ Recreation
- ✓ Animation
- ✓ Transportation
- ✓ Exploration
- ✓ Engineering

- ✓ Architecture
- ✓ Design
- ✓ Fashion
- ✓ Parks
- ✓ Rides
- ✓ Toys
- ✓ Video Games
- ✓ Technology
- ✓ Robots
- ✓ Inventions

We pay a premium for these things so we can experience the fruits of mankind's *play!*

Play is the true source of all the immeasurable value we've injected into this world. It's the DNA of our culture, and the backbone of our global economy. All the world-shaking creativity, profitable innovations, fulfilling jobs, and beloved magic that we've conjured throughout the ages has come from the freedom to have our own fun, for hours and weeks and years on end.

I've met a lot of incredibly talented and successful people. Guess what: Nearly all of them approach their lives this way – *they play*. No one forces them to work on things they don't care about, or tells them how to spend their time. They just give themselves permission to follow their impulses and pursue what excites them. They create a little universe that revolves around their own fun.

Instead of grinding it out in jobs they hate, these people become passionate and highly skilled at what they do. They team up with other great players and collaborate on interesting projects. Then one day, they're making magic. Their mastery shines through in everything they create, society reaps the benefits of their gifts, and our world changes.

Need proof? Just listen to some of the most revered and accomplished members of society, who all chose to play for a living:

I never did a day's work in my life. It was all fun.

— THOMAS EDISON

—〰—

Play is the highest form of research.

— ALBERT EINSTEIN

—〰—

The only way to do great work is to love what you do.

— STEVE JOBS

———

The work that is really a man's own work is play and not work at all... When we talk about the great workers of the world, we really mean the great players of the world.

— MARK TWAIN

———

I just write what I wanted to write. I write what amuses me. It's totally for myself.

— J.K. ROWLING

———

I dream for a living.

— STEVEN SPIELBERG

———

*We believed in our idea: a family park where parents
and children could have fun, together.*

— WALT DISNEY

—⧟—

In every real man a child is hidden that wants to play.

— FRIEDRICH NIETZSCHE

—⧟—

*I found child's play — stuff that was not considered
serious, but goofy — was the stuff I liked to do, so I
still do it as an adult.*

— MATT GROENING

—⧟—

*I always try to create new experiences that are
fun to play.*

— SHIGERU MIYAMOTO

—⧟—

I loved to make people laugh in high school, and then I found I loved being on stage in front of people.

— STEVE MARTIN

—⚋—

I learned how important it is to entertain people and give them a reason to come and watch you play.

— ELVIS PRESLEY

—⚋—

The Beatles saved the world from boredom.

— GEORGE HARRISON

—⚋—

Take the job you would take if you were independently wealthy. You're going to do well at it. [5]

— WARREN BUFFETT

—⚋—

---

[5] If you'd like to share any of these quotes, go to playitaway.me/quotes.

What's money? A man is a success if he gets up in the morning and goes to bed at night and in between does what he wants to do.

— BOB DYLAN

—⚏—

My general attitude to life is to enjoy every minute of every day. I never do anything with a feeling of, 'Oh God, I've got to do this today.'

— RICHARD BRANSON

—⚏—

My life has no purpose, no direction, no aim, no meaning, and yet I'm happy. I can't figure it out. What am I doing right?

— CHARLES M. SCHULZ

—⚏—

My motto is: more good times.

— JACK NICHOLSON

—⚡—

Life well spent is long.

— LEONARDO DA VINCI

—⚡—

Life's like a movie, write your own ending. Keep believing, keep pretending.

— JIM HENSON

—⚡—

Just play. Have fun. Enjoy the game.

— MICHAEL JORDAN

—⚡—

Man is God's plaything, and that is the best part of him.

Therefore every man and woman should live life

accordingly, and play the noblest games...

What, then, is the right way of living?

Life must be lived as play.

— PLATO

Best of all, play utterly *destroys* anxiety! It smothers our worries by allowing us to have fun with other people. Play is the social grease that makes us a part of the group, which prevents us from feeling alone and afraid. It's the harmonious common ground that brings us all together, and allows us to act as one.

None of us were ever supposed to feel alone or afraid in the first place! The people who try to convince you that life has to be that way just aren't very good at playing. They've forgotten what it's like. But we all want to have fun and be happy together. We all want to connect. So have a laugh, remind them that it's okay, and just play.

You don't need more money. You don't need more free time. You can always do it.

Play is a state of mind – it's a way to approach the world. Whether your world is a frightening prison or a loving playground is entirely up to you.

It's only a choice: Anxiety or Play.

Take your pick.[6]

---

[6] If you're ready to start playing more, skip ahead to the section *Enjoy Guilt-Free Play with Friends* (page 70).

5

MY 4-WEEK PLAN FOR HEALTH AND HAPPINESS

Viewing the world through the lens of *Play* allowed me to enjoy life again, but it didn't heal my anxiety overnight. I still felt tense and worried, and I was out of touch with my friends. But for the first time in more than a year, I had a glimmer of hope. And within one month of viewing my life as *Play*, I was back to my old self.

This section of the book contains every technique I used to heal my anxious mind, control my workaholism, and improve the quality of my life. Everything I'm going to recommend did wonders for my mental, emotional, and physical well being. Practicing these techniques on a regular basis made me happier than I'd felt in years.

Here's the general outline of my 4-week plan for health and

happiness:

Week (1) - Remove Your Anchors
Week (2) - Heal Your Mind
Week (3) - Heal Your Body
Week (4) - Heal Your World

If you'd like to follow along with my 4-week plan, **I highly recommend that you go one week at a time**. Don't skip ahead, and don't try every technique all at once. That kind of drastic alteration to your schedule will fall apart in a matter of days. I know you're desperate to feel better *right now*, but the plan works best when you go one week at a time.

Also, during weeks 2-4, you don't have to practice every technique I recommend. You can always pick ONE that sounds like it could really improve your life, give it a shot for seven days, and then assess how you feel at the end. If it's clearly working, stick with it. If not, try another technique.

Are you ready? It's time to get your life back.

> *Perfection is achieved not when there is*
> *nothing more to add, but when there is*
> *nothing left to take away.*
>
> — ANTOINE DE SAINT-EXUPERY

Pretend you're sitting in a boat in the middle of a lake. You want to paddle to shore, but there's a problem – your boat has several anchors attached to it. Should you paddle as hard and fast as you can, or should you stop and remove the anchors?

Obviously, you need to remove the anchors before you can start paddling. Otherwise you're going to work ten times harder than necessary, and you won't make any real progress. Or worse, you might even sink.

The same principle applies to your anxiety. You need to cast off the emotional weights that are dragging you down before you can lift yourself back up.

In order to heal your anxiety and start viewing your life as

Play, you must *Remove Your Anchors*. These are the stressors that continually thrust you into heightened states of emotional strain. It's very easy to tolerate these sources of stress, day after day, always feeling unhappy. But if you truly want to get back to a healthy state of mind, you must identify and remove your anchors as completely as possible.

Before I jump into the specifics of the *Remove Your Anchors* exercise, I want to show you my four heaviest anchors, along with the solutions I implemented to get rid of them. Hopefully, this will increase your awareness of the things that might be weighing you down.

ANCHOR ①: FEAR OF GETTING ATTACKED

SOLUTION: STOP READING AND WATCHING THE NEWS

Learning to ignore things is one of the great

paths to inner peace.

— ROBERT J. SAWYER

It took me a long time to see it, but *the news* was my single biggest source of anxiety. The websites I was reading each day talked non-stop about crime, corruption, economic breakdown, and the end of the world. As a result, my fear of being attacked spun out of control. I became obsessed with protecting myself from every possible threat to my livelihood. I researched what to do if I was arrested and thrown in jail. I spent hundreds of dollars on food and equipment that I hoped would save me in the event of a disaster.

There was nothing inherently wrong with preparing for an emergency, but obsessing over preposterous apocalyptic scenarios, every single day, for months on end? What an enormous waste of time and energy!

After I did the *Remove Your Anchors* exercise, it finally dawned on me: **my fear of an imaginary future was destroying my**

ability to enjoy the present.

And what planted those seeds of fear? *The news.*

When I made the commitment to cut the news out of my life completely, my anxiety plummeted in less than two weeks. The negative information I removed from my conscious awareness freed me from the confines of other people's frightening narratives.

I replaced the scary news with positive, joyful, and fun information. For instance, I listened to uplifting songs and standup comedy albums. I watched funny and happy movies. I read fiction books that sparked my imagination (rather than workaholic business books that made me feel productive). It really helped.[7]

Of course, I didn't bury my head in the sand. I still talked with my friends, who would inevitably bring up the noteworthy events that took place that week. And I was always surprised to discover that... *I didn't really miss anything.* I was alive, and the world kept turning. That was about it.

---

[7] For a list of my favorite anxiety-fighting content, visit playitaway.me/antinews. Just remember: Sad people tend to focus on the lyrics, while happy people just listen to the music. Don't over-analyze the deeper implications of the content; just enjoy how it makes you feel.

The information you allow into your conscious awareness determines the quality of your life. In other words, you are what you think. If you are subsisting on content that's unsettling, anxious, and soulless (see: the news, reality shows, horror movies, books written by hateful authors, porn), your mind will become stressed, scared, and cynical. But if you are consuming content that's joyous and playful, your mind will become happy and loving.

Do not hesitate to cut anxiety-inducing information — especially the news – out of your daily routine completely! If your friends are watching the news in the same room, either change the channel or go do something else. If a scary headline appears in your Facebook feed, don't click it – block it!

There's no need to subject yourself to unhealthy unrealities.[8] Replace those unsettling thoughts with positive content that will lift you up. Otherwise, you will taint your thoughts, instill fear in your mind, and continually spoil the quality of your life.

---

[8] For those who think it's their civic duty to stay up-to-date on world affairs… Bear in mind that almost every source of news makes their money through *advertisements*. In order to stay in business and earn a profit, these news outlets need as many people to see their ads as possible. And because they're all selling the same

ANCHOR ②: FEAR OF HAVING A PANIC ATTACK

SOLUTION: STOP DRINKING RIDICULOUS AMOUNTS OF CAFFEINE

 The physical sensations that preceded my panic attacks were the jitters (shaking hands, quivering voice) and a rapid resting heart rate. Guess what gave me both of those sensations? Coffee. And wouldn't you know it, I was drinking 3-4 cups each day, running around like Tweek on *South Park.*

I decided to cut coffee out of my diet for a week. Shortly after

product, they have to fight each other for your attention *every single minute*. The way the news earns your attention is NOT by providing you with useful or accurate information, but by shocking you with sensationalist headlines and artificial drama. In other words, the only way the news knows how to stay in business is by winding all of us up. We're especially profitable for them when we are collectively terrified or enraged. Terrorist attack? *Cha-ching!* Non-stop coverage!

The sad truth is that news outlets no longer care about investigative reporting, biased agendas, relevant information, facts, or whether they're poisoning their audience's psyche. All they care about is numbers: page views, shares, and eyeballs for their ads. Even the "truth deliverers" and conspiracy websites play this game. It's an impossible undertaking to sort through their incessant distortion of reality, and you can never be sure if what you're reading is true... But that's not what this book is about. All I can say is that the news was making me afraid of the world. When I cut it out, I stopped being afraid. You are free to do the same.

I removed the caffeine from my bloodstream, I stopped having the jitters. My resting heart rate remained steady. The physical sensations that came with a panic attack were no longer there, and I started calming down.[9]

A friend of mine experienced something similar. She had horrible anxiety for months but couldn't figure out what was causing it. One day at work, she noticed that she'd finished three diet sodas in just a few hours. Her body was overloaded with caffeine and aspartame (a poisonous chemical in diet drinks that is 100% legal). As soon as she stopped drinking diet soda, her anxiety disappeared.

Every chemical you're regularly ingesting is being absorbed in your bloodstream, which is potentially having a HUGE impact on your anxiety. You might be used to consuming stimulants to stay awake (or drinking/smoking to calm down), but if your body keeps freaking out, it's signaling that something is wrong. This should be obvious, but we tend to overlook the simple answers that are right in front of us.

Cut out any substance you regularly consume that's correlated with increased feelings of anxiety. Common culprits include: caffeine, aspartame, refined sugar, alcohol,

---

[9] After some experimentation, I found that I could only have a half serving of coffee before I started feeling jittery. I also discovered that I couldn't have caffeine past 5:00PM without disrupting my sleep.

cigarettes, and marijuana. Keep it out of your body for one week.

If you have that substance in your house, throw it away. If the people you spend the most time with are encouraging you to consume it, politely turn them down and do something else. If you have strong cravings for that substance, find a healthy substitute you can consume instead.

After the substance has been out of your system for seven days, you can reassess its toxicity by consuming a typical dose you're used to taking. If your anxiety symptoms return within one hour of ingestion, you've found the culprit. Try to eliminate that substance for good.

ANCHOR (3): FEELING ANXIOUS AROUND CERTAIN PEOPLE

SOLUTION: STOP SPENDING TIME WITH VAMPIRES

You are the average of the five people
you spend the most time with.

— JIM ROHN

My first relationship was in 5th grade. I'd never felt so stressed out in my life. There were all these rules and restrictions I had to obey. I needed to hold my girlfriend's hand in class.

I needed to hang out with her at recess. I needed to call her after school. I couldn't talk to other girls. The whole ordeal was exhausting.

My mom noticed how unhappy I was, and asked if I'd considered ending the relationship. "I can do that?" I exclaimed, amazed that I wasn't shackled to my new existence. The next day, I made the break with these immortalized words: "You're dumped."

Of course, we were just kids. Neither of us knew what we were doing, so we tortured ourselves by being really serious around each other. Shortly after we broke up, we were able to relax, joke around, and have fun again.

When I was at the peak of my anxiety, I noticed those same feelings from my first relationship kept cropping up around certain people. I felt worried, tense, serious, or angry every time we interacted. But I wasn't dating any of these people. They were just a whirlwind of stress that I kept getting caught up in.

After I did the *Remove Your Anchors* exercise, I decided to cut the vampires out of my life. I know the term "vampires" sounds like a goofy self-help cliché, but it was a useful label for identifying the people who were fueling my anxiety.

A vampire is someone who drains your energy when you interact with them. You can recognize a vampire just by recognizing your body's overwhelmingly negative responses to them. When you get a message from a vampire, your stomach drops. When you're hanging out with a vampire, you feel tense and angry. When you leave a vampire's presence, you feel relieved and exhausted. When you run into a vampire in public, your first impulse is to avoid eye contact and hide.

Like all human beings, vampires have redeemable qualities. But their positive traits are heavily outweighed by how weak, afraid, and awful you feel around them. You can never relax or be yourself around a vampire, because you're too busy trying to avoid their emotional assault. Vampires fuel your anxiety, and at some point, you need to say "Enough."

When I finally acknowledged how weak and anxious the vampires in my life made me feel, I decided to stop spending time with them. I didn't explain myself or tell them they were the problem; I just stopped making their happiness my priority and cut off communication. After a few weeks of turning down meetups and ignoring messages, they slowly began to fade away.[10]

---

[10] Yes, it's selfish to dismiss people. But selfishness is a virtue when it makes you a better person. Constantly accommodating unhappiness and bad feelings - just so two people can be in the same room together - is a waste of everyone's time and energy.

While I was ignoring the vampires, I focused on spending more time with people *I genuinely loved being around*. People who were easygoing, upbeat, funny, and loving. Being around positive friends, who didn't try to control or change my behavior, naturally brought out my authentic playful self. We felt safe and secure around each other because our only priority was just to have fun together. Positive people had the inverse effect of vampires; they *replenished* my energy, and *reduced* my anxiety. The more time I spent around them, the better I felt. It really was that simple.

Anyone who consistently drains your energy and makes you feel weak is a vampire. Even if they are a longtime friend, a co-worker, a significant other, or a blood relative, *a vampire is still a vampire*. It's important to acknowledge how awful they make you feel so you can start consciously limiting your time with them. Otherwise, they will keep thrusting you into heightened states of panic, anger, and sadness.

Don't try to change a vampire's behavior (it doesn't work[11]), and don't worry so much about *their* happiness. Look out for yourself by limiting your time with them, or cut them out of your life completely.

---

[11] Some people change, of course, and you can always give them another shot. But true change must come from within. You can't command someone to be a different person; they have to want to change first, and then make it happen on their own terms.

ANCHOR (4): TRYING TO LIVE UP TO PEOPLE'S EXPECTATIONS

SOLUTION: STOP DOING WORK THAT DOESN'T MATTER TO YOU

It was pretty stressful quitting two cool gigs (Tim Ferriss' assistant, co-founder of a startup) within a matter of months. I felt spoiled and embarrassed whenever I had to explain why I'd left – *I had no desire to do the work.* I wasn't interested in what I was doing anymore, and no amount of money or prestige could excite me enough to work on things I didn't want to work on.

And yet, I still felt obligated to live up to people's expectations. Everyone asked me about my future and what I was going to do next. And there was this voice in my head that kept telling me how far I'd come, and now I was blowing it. I needed to be a rich entrepreneur, or a CEO of a startup, or someone who'd changed the world in order for everyone to permanently accept that I was successful.

This pressure I felt to *make it* was such a burden, until I realized that I would never be content. I'd be working harder and harder just so I could keep regaining everyone's approval. No level of success would ever be enough because I would always be chasing the world outside of me. What was the point of working so hard if I wasn't doing it for myself?

The solution for removing this anchor became very clear: **stop doing work that doesn't matter to you.**[12]

You might roll your eyes at this. *I can't quit my job! No one is hiring! The economy is terrible! I have a family and bills to pay!* I understand. You don't have to quit everything you don't want to work on right away. You just have to start working on projects you actually care about. Here's how I did it...

The first step was to change how I thought about work. Rather than viewing work as a stressful obligation or a means of getting rich, *my work was just a game I was choosing to play.* This subtle shift immediately snapped me out of my bad habit of accepting work I didn't care about.

During the months prior, my days were spent working on email campaigns, running P.R. and social media for random clients, and a bunch of stuff I had zero interest in doing. I was just so caught up in the money and my own sense of importance that I kept overlooking how much I disliked the work itself.

---

[12] **Warning:** Quitting work you don't care about is a fantastic long term decision. However, quitting may intensify your anxiety if you don't know what to replace your old job with. Try to have an enjoyable alternative lined up before you make the leap. And if your alternative doesn't work out, don't give up. Keep experimenting with your work conditions and trying things that interest you until you find a mix that's fun and rewarding.

I wanted my work to be a game I would willingly play, so I thought back on my *Play History* (the activities I repeatedly turned to throughout my life because they were fun and I was good at them):[13]

✓ Creating my own art (film, writing)
✓ Making people laugh (performing, comedy, pranks)
✓ Learning and developing skills
✓ Team sports (playing with fun people)
✓ Building and fixing things with my hands

I wanted to spend more of my time doing these things. Those were the games that truly mattered to me. I gave myself a new rule: **Any project I pursued had to be aligned with my Play History.** In other words, all of my work had to allow me to create my own art, make people laugh, develop my skills, play with fun people, or build something with my hands. If the gig didn't meet my criteria, then I would turn it down.

It was *my life*, and I wanted to play *my games*. If other people didn't like my games or how I played them, no problem! There were plenty of desperate job-hunters who were willing to play by someone else's rules. For me, the work had to be its own reward.

---

[13] If you want to discover your own Play History, skip ahead to *Enjoy Guilt-Free Play with Friends* (page 70).

I started setting aside 20 minutes each day to work on a project I cared about. This ensured that I was regularly practicing my favorite games, even if I wasn't being paid. The project could be as small as repairing a leaky sink, or drawing a funny picture, or practicing guitar... Giving myself at least 20 minutes each day to work on something personally rewarding was enough to make me *happy*.

I kept brainstorming ways to make money through my favorite games. I already knew the formula:

Solve a big problem that you and a lot of other people have

Create the best possible solution

+ Charge for your solution

Profit!

I'd already solved some of my biggest problems, and I was an expert in a few areas that a lot of people needed help with. And because creating art was one of my favorite games, I decided to write a couple of books on those topics. Look, you're reading one of those books right now!

Work shouldn't feel like indentured servitude; it should feel like a game you would willingly play because it's rewarding and it energizes you. The good news is that your work can be a game, so long as you allow yourself to view it through that lens. All you need to do is give yourself permission to have fun by working on things you enjoy each day.

Continually putting up with work that you hate is a path that leads to unhappiness and regret. If you find yourself spending months or years working on things you dislike — due to your fear of quitting someone else's game — it's probably time to rethink how you want to live your life.

Now it's time for you to try the *Remove Your Anchors* exercise. This will be critical to your success in curing your anxiety. Once you've removed your top sources of stress, a path will be cleared in your mind. The energy you spent dragging those anchors around can then be used to lift yourself back up. When you reach that point, you'll be able to heal yourself in a matter of weeks.

PART I – IDENTIFY YOUR ANCHORS

Grab a pen and piece of paper. Spend the next 5-10 minutes writing down everything you worry about on a daily and weekly basis. Think of all the things that consistently drain your energy or make you feel anxious, and jot them down.

Don't go into too much detail; just write 3-5 words per item. For instance: lack of exercise, being around [vampire's name], panic attacks, etc.

After you're finished, look back at your list. There are probably a couple things that really stand out as your top sources of stress...

Put a star next to your 1-2 heaviest anchors. These are the biggest stressors that you'll want to work on relieving and/or removing first.

PART 2 - REMOVE YOUR ANCHORS

Now it's time to frame your 1-2 heaviest anchors as "How can I eliminate" questions. For instance...

If your heaviest anchor is "loneliness," you would frame it as:

> How can I eliminate my loneliness?

If your heaviest anchor is "student loans," you would frame it as:

> How can I eliminate my student loans?

You might be laughing already. *Impossible*, you say. I get it.

But before you jump into armchair critic mode and reject this as a futile exercise, you need to actually TRY IT.

Remember: Countless people have experienced and *triumphed over* the things that are stressing you out right now. The difference between you and them is that they removed their anchors intentionally and strategically. They figured out a game plan and put it into action, rather than sitting around feeling helpless. That's why you need to do this exercise – it will force you to brainstorm ways to make your life better.

After each *How can I eliminate* question, you should jot down three potential solutions that you think could remove that anchor. Your solutions don't have to be perfect; you're just trying to come up with something. Write down your "How can I eliminate" question for your heaviest anchor (or two), and your three potential solutions like so:

HOW CAN I ELIMINATE _____ ?

(1) _____

(2) _____

(3) _____

Put a star next to the <u>simplest solution</u> you come up with. A great simple solution will be: (A) small and uncomplicated,

(B) fun and exciting to implement, and (C) easy to stick with.

For instance, the simple solution I came up with for my fear of being attacked was to cut out the news. This worked because it was straightforward, enjoyable (I replaced the news with happier content), and a painless change for me to make.

Same deal with my fear of having a panic attacks. My simple solution for removing that anchor was to eliminate caffeine. The solution was clear, rewarding, and relatively effortless (I replaced coffee with water).

Once you have your own simple solution, put it into action *immediately* to see how effective it is for removing that anchor. If your simple solution hasn't noticeably alleviated your anxiety within one week, try your second best solution the following week. Keep experimenting until you hit upon a solution that removes (or significantly relieves) your heaviest anchor within one week. The process won't always be easy or quick, but it is absolutely worth the effort.

Continue doing this exercise once each week. Set a reminder to *Remove Your Anchors* every Sunday. When you really commit to this exercise, your brain automatically shifts from *Why me?* to *Let's take action!* Suddenly, you're no longer paralyzed; you are setting yourself in motion. And as a result, your anxiety goes down, your energy goes up, and your life is already 1% better.

END OF WEEK I - ASSESSMENT

✓ Did you write down all the things you worry about on a daily and weekly basis?

✓ Did you pinpoint your 1-2 heaviest anchors?

✓ Did you put your simple solution(s) into action?

✓ Were your heaviest anchors reduced or removed?

On a scale of 0 - 100%, how much did your anxiety drop this week?

After my heaviest anchors were removed, my mind was no longer consumed with worry. I regained a ton of energy, which I re-directed to activities that made me feel happy and healthy.

That's what the next three weeks of the plan are going to cover: *the anxiety-healing techniques that really worked for me.*

WEEK 2 - HEAL YOUR MIND

1. *Enjoy Guilt-Free Play With Friends*
2. *Consistent Bedtime & 20-Minute Naps*
3. *Observe Your Thoughts*

ENJOY GUILT-FREE PLAY
WITH FRIENDS

Let's go fly a kite.

— Mary Poppins

Playing on a regular basis is an investment in your health and happiness. Not only does it allow you to have fun with your friends while exercising, it also turns your thoughts off for a while so your brain can recharge. Reducing your anxiety through play only takes 2% of your total time each week (that's 30 minutes every day), but it's up to you to decide that your happiness is worth the effort.

If you're ready to play more but aren't sure where to start, the first thing you should do is create your *Play History*.[14] Here's how:

Recall as many of the fun activities that you repeatedly and voluntarily turned to during your childhood, and write them all down.

I spent about 20 minutes writing down everything I could

---

[14] This idea comes from the book *Play* by Dr. Stuart Brown.

recall from my own *Play History*. Then I called up a few childhood friends to ask what games they remembered us playing together when we were growing up.

My top five *Play History* activities were:

- ✓ Creating my own art (film, writing)
- ✓ Making people laugh (improv comedy, pranks[15])
- ✓ Learning and developing new skills (guitar)
- ✓ Team sports (catch, home run derby)
- ✓ Building and fixing things with my hands

After my list was complete, I set aside dedicated time for my favorite play activities in my daily schedule. That's right - I actually scheduled a recurring event in my calendar called *Play!* I know this technically goes against the spontaneous nature of playing, but I'm a recovering workaholic. Cut me some slack.

Each weekend, my friends and I played home run derby

---

[15] Anyone can pull great pranks if they're equipped with super glue, duct tape, water balloons, an air horn, and/or a hidden camera. My personal favorite prank is to leave Chick-Fil-A mayonnaise packets under toilet seat bumpers. The results are breathtaking.

(which I hadn't played in almost nine years). For me, that was the most rewarding form of play. Taking batting practice was always so much fun, and it gave me an excuse to move around outdoors for a couple hours.

I also started taking frequent trips to the park with an Aerobie Flying Ring (a flat rubber Frisbee that flies really fast). The Aerobie was perfect for playing catch because I had to call up a friend to join me, and we'd both end up running around while chasing it.

We're phasing out the games. People drink less when they're having fun.

— MOE, THE SIMPSONS

Incorporating play into my weekly routine helped my anxiety and workaholism more than anything else. It was such a massive relief to hang out with my friends and have guilt-free fun again. Playing helped me decompress and unplug from work, which actually made me more productive.

After each round of catch or home run derby, I would return to my laptop feeling light and happy. And to my surprise, I was able to produce better work at a faster pace. My brain was operating at a higher level because it was happy, playful, and recharged.

I wasn't the only one. Two of my close friends attested to a boost in productivity and creativity because of play. My friend Ann (a book editor) texted me one afternoon to say that she was trying to work, but was so bored that she'd spent the last hour staring at a turtle swimming in a pond. I told her to come pick me up so we could play catch. We drove over to a park and played with the Aerobie for two hours in the sun. The next day, she sent me this message:

> It's amazing how giving myself a day to play (or acquiescing that I could only play?) yesterday has made working today so much easier

My friend Erin (a graphic designer) experienced similar results from playing. Ann and I called her one night to see if she wanted to hang out. Erin said there was no way she could, as she'd missed the deadline for a client's website. Ann and I heard the frustration in her voice and decided to drive over to her apartment.

When we arrived, Erin was freaking out and completely

exhausted. She was barely halfway finished, and had at least six more hours of work left. Erin weakly declared she was going to stay up all night to get the site done.

Ann and I forced Erin to quit work for the night so she could come play mini golf. She was a bit stressed out by the kidnapping, but she loosened up by the time we arrived at the course. The three of us goofed around for a couple hours, giving each other a hard time at each hole, and laughing like maniacs with every inappropriate joke we told. By the end of the night, we were all happy and relaxed.

The next day, Erin told us how much better she felt after taking some time off to play. She went straight to bed when she got back home, had a good night's rest, and was able to finish the site in *less than two hours* the next morning. **Play, it seemed, had the power to make our work easier, faster, and more enjoyable.**

All work and no play makes Jack a dull boy. So if you aren't dedicating enough time to *play* with your friends, schedule it in your calendar. Seriously. Start by playing at least twice a week, for a minimum of 30 minutes per session.

If you're having trouble coming up with your own *Play History*, call up a few of your childhood friends and ask for their input. You can also refer to these lists of play activities for inspiration:[16]

SOLO ACTIVITY

- Archery
- Batting cages
- Biking
- Boogie boarding
- Building things with your hands
- Coloring books
- Cooking
- Creating art
- Driving range
- Fishing
- Ice skating
- Kite flying
- K'Nex
- Legos
- Lifting weights
- Long boarding
- Painting
- Playing an instrument
- Playing with dogs
- Reading fiction
- Rock climbing
- Roller skating
- Running
- Skateboarding
- Skiing
- Snowboarding
- Swimming
- Surfing
- Woodworking
- Writing for fun
- Yoga

2-4 PEOPLE

- Billiards
- Bowling
- Boxing
- Camping
- Catch
- Dance lessons
- Darts
- Disc golf
- Filming sketches
- Frisbee

[16] To see a visual list of play activities, visit playitaway.me/fun.

- Golf
- Hiking
- Home run derby
- H.O.R.S.E.
- Making music
- Mario Kart 64
- Martial arts
- Ping pong
- Poker
- Power lifting
- Pranks

- Racquetball
- Road trip
- Sailing
- Scavenger hunt
- Swings
- Tennis
- Trampoline
- Tubing
- Wake boarding
- Wii Bowling

BIG GROUPS

- Amusement Parks
- Baseball
- Basketball
- Beach volleyball
- Cricket
- Co-ed team sports
- Dance parties
- Dodgeball
- Football
- Handball
- Hockey
- Improv comedy classes
- Kickball
- Lacrosse

- Partying
- Rugby
- Slip-N-Slide
- Soccer
- Softball
- Squash
- TP'ing houses
- Ultimate Frisbee
- Volleyball
- Water balloon fights
- Water polo
- White water rafting
- Wiffle ball

In my experience, the best forms of anxiety-reducing play are *outdoor sports*. They are social (more than one person is required), mildly competitive, and cause everyone to break a sweat in the fresh air and sunshine. However, any fun play activity that you can do on a regular basis with your friends should work.[17]

You can take baby steps toward playing more, of course. You could invite a friend on a long walk, or play catch instead of drinking coffee, or take a date to the driving range. **The important thing is to make time for guilt-free fun with good people.**

Isolating yourself from people erodes your health, and sitting in a chair all day long is a recipe for neuroses. Get off the internet, turn off your screens, and go have guilt-free fun playing with your friends! You'll be less anxious, less lonely, more relaxed, and a whole lot happier.

---

[17] Just to reiterate: the best forms of play are physically active, mildly competitive, and require you to interact with your friends face-to-face. Video games can technically fall into that category, but they are usually a solo activity where you're sitting alone indoors, staring at a screen for hours on end. Just because you're playing *Call of Duty* or *Candy Crush* all the time doesn't mean you're actually playing.

THREE RULES FOR PROPER PLAY

Rule 1

DISCONNECT FROM SOCIAL MEDIA

I know people will still be tempted to do this even after an explicit warning, but **you need to disconnect from social media in order to play.**

This is the time to bond with your friends. It is NOT the time to show how great your life is to people who aren't even there. Constantly taking pictures for Instagram or updating your Facebook destroys the spontaneous nature of play. Rather than being in the moment and having fun, you're just distracting yourself with the thought of how many Likes and comments your updates are getting.

If you truly want to get your anxiety and workaholism under control, you need to disconnect. If the lure of the internet is too tempting, just turn your cell phone OFF.

I know it's fun to share your life, but social media is destructive when it's compulsively used to gloss over how lonely and insecure you feel. Stop trying to convince everyone that you have a perfect life. Face the fact that you *don't,* then go play so you can make it better.

Rule 2

HARMONY > WINNING

If you played competitive sports growing up, you were probably conditioned to take winning very seriously. Each year, the games became more serious, prestigious, and competitive. For me, I graduated from playing catch with my dad, to street games with my friends, to Little League, to Apache League, to high school tryouts, to Varsity. But by the time I was 18 years old, I'd lost interest in every sport because only "the best" were allowed on the field. I got so fed up with the seriousness of the coaches and the drills and the wins that I was ready to quit. The spirit of play was scrubbed out of the games.[18]

Fortunately, the competitive sports world is not the play world. Anyone who wants to play can be included, no matter how sloppy or unskilled they are. **That's because play is NOT about winning or being the best; it's about harmony.** Tone down your cutthroat competitive streak and relentless

---

[18] This dynamic made sports unnecessarily dramatic and miserable. As a result, I have very little patience watching professional sports. It's not fun for me to sit around yelling at people who take their games way too seriously.

desire to dominate.[19] Those traits are counter-productive, and they're a buzz kill for your friends. Give yourself permission to relax, fail, and lose.

Rule 3

HAVE F*ING FUN!

*I play real sports. I'm not trying to be
the best at working out.*

— KENNY POWERS

Exercise is a proven way to reduce stress and depression. But what's the best type of exercise? Running on the treadmill for an hour? Doing hundreds of sit-ups? Self-inflicted torture via P90X?

How about 'None of the Above'? All of those activities are lame and miserable. People only do them because they think getting in shape has to be a punishment.

Exercise should not feel like *work*; it should be *play*. In other words, physical movement that gets your heart racing, causes you to sweat, and is legitimately fun for you and your friends.

---

[19] If you can't help but take play seriously, you'll need to find other playmates who act the same way and can compete on your level.

If you want to be healthier and happier, you should start thinking of exercise as an opportunity to Play. You don't have to track your time, measure your heart rate, or count your calories. Forget that noise. Just focus on having fun while moving around with your friends.

FREQUENCY: Aim for 30 minutes per day (or more, if possible).

COST: Free, or very cheap. Try not to think of play in terms of costs. This is an investment in your health and happiness, with a guaranteed return.

DO IT NOW: Write down your *Play History*. Schedule a daily reminder in your calendar to Play! Ask a friend, co-worker, or neighbor to play catch for 10 minutes.

RESOURCES: ***Play: How it Shapes the Brain, Opens the Imagination, and Invigorates the Soul* (playitaway.me/play)** If you want to read more about the science behind play and its essential role in fueling happiness, pick up a copy of this book. It's fantastic.

Aerobie Flying Ring (playitaway.me/ aerobie) This is the best toy for playing catch. It's light, durable, portable, and extremely fun.

Charlie's Play Picks (playitaway.me/ fun) Check out the entire list of my favorite activities, toys to play with, and fun places to play.

Local Play. Search Yelp.com for "co-ed sports" or "improv comedy," then sign up! For a negligible fee, you get to be surrounded by fun people who like to play. Totally worth it.

BONUS POINTS

15-MINUTES OF SUN AND FRESH AIR

I grew up in Colorado, a beautiful state with 300 days of sunshine each year. As a kid, I spent a ton of time outdoors, and always had easy access to fresh air and natural vitamin D. But when I moved to a major city, I found myself in a shadowy concrete jungle. I was surrounded by tall buildings, and spent the majority of my days indoors, seldom feeling the warmth of the sun. The air was permeated with an array of foreign smells, like truck fumes and homeless people's feces.

A lot of my friends love living in big cities, like New York and Los Angeles. Personally, it drove me nuts. The noise and chaos are incessant, and it's really difficult to get adequate sunlight and fresh air. I realized I wasn't getting enough of either in downtown San Francisco, so I came up with a few workarounds.

For starters, I would stand on the patio each morning with my shirt off,[20] trying to absorb the sun for at least 15 minutes. I was also taking 2,000 IU's (two drops) of liquid Vitamin D-3 each day.

For fresh air, I left the windows in my apartment open to increase the circulation, kept an air purifier running in my bedroom, and left the city for a nature hike each weekend.

Currently, I'm living in Austin, Texas. Each day, I spend a minimum of 15-30 minutes out in the sun and fresh air (again, no shirt). I don't put on sunscreen; I just absorb the sun's rays until it feels like I've had enough.[21] It's just as effective as caffeine for charging up on energy.

---

[20] Most females aren't too comfortable going bare up there. Throw on a swimsuit top if you don't want to shock your neighbors.

[21] *But don't you worry about skin cancer?!* No, because I listen to what my body is telling me. When my skin feels like it's had enough sun, I put on my shirt and go back inside. I don't get burned because I don't stay out for an excessive amount of time, which sunscreen often tricks me into doing.

It's insane to me that we are the only species that wears clothes. We are all blocking our skin from having access to air and sunlight on a daily basis! Try to expose your body to the elements for at least 15 minutes each day. Let the sun warm your skin, and the wind flick your pores. It's good for you.

If you're a workaholic, you're probably spending your days in a temperature-controlled room with artificial lighting and poor air circulation. These conditions are foreign for human beings. You need to get outdoors so you can get some sun and fresh air, whether it's through play or just laying out in the grass. You'll have more energy, you'll feel happier, and you'll look healthier.

FREQUENCY: Daily, at least 15 minutes.

COST: Free.

DO IT NOW: Put on your swimsuit. Go outdoors in the fresh air and sunshine for 15 minutes.

RESOURCES: **Now Liquid Vitamin D-3 (playitaway. me/vitamind)** [This is not an affiliate link.] I was taking 2,000 IU's (two drops) each day.

Honeywell Compact Air purifier (playitaway.me/air) If you're living in a big city, you're probably not getting much fresh air. The best option is to put an air purifier in the room you spend the most time in. Honeywell's is low maintenance and it captures mold, pollen, smoke, pet dander, and dust particles.

CONSISTENT BEDTIME AND AFTERNOON NAPS

My girlfriend asked me, 'Did you sleep good?'
I said 'No, I made a few mistakes.'

— STEVEN WRIGHT

Back in high school, I was obsessed with getting great sleep. I moved to the cool basement in my parents' house, covered the windows with layers of black construction paper, and ran a desk fan to drown out disruptive noises. My sleep was amazing every night.

As I grew older, sleep became less of a priority. I did a lot of all-nighters in college and got used to going to bed at random hours – usually between 3:00 and 7:00AM.[22] My erratic sleep schedule continued long after graduating. I worked around the clock, drank coffee all day, consumed junk food and alcohol late at night, and checked my bright cell phone screen while I was in bed. Then I'd wake up a few hours later and do it all over again. And what a shock: *I felt exhausted all the time.*

---

[22] My roommate once called me "the Chuck Norris of all-nighters." Not a good thing.

I was chronically in a severe sleep deficit, which took a major toll on my body. But I kept ignoring my fatigue because I felt guilty whenever I wasn't working. To me, sleep was a necessary evil that cut into my productivity.

The endless stream of digital information I was taking in every waking hour only compounded the problem. My mind never had enough time to shut down, relax, and digest everything that poured in during the day. No wonder my mental health was shot.

During the month I cured my anxiety, I made consistent sleep one of my highest priorities. The first thing I did was **optimize my bedroom for ideal sleeping conditions.** Here are the steps I took:

(1) Plugged my iPhone charger in an outlet far away from my bed so I couldn't grab my phone while I was laying down. This little obstacle prevented me from checking email or Facebook before trying to fall asleep.

(2) Cranked up the air conditioning so the temperature in my bedroom was around 68 degrees Fahrenheit.[23]

---

[23] To ensure I never felt too warm at night, I only slept in gym shorts.

③ Kept the curtains drawn and wore a sleep mask so that my room was as dark as I could possibly make it.

④ Downloaded the Relax Melodies app, which played a continuous loop of ocean waves throughout the night.

Once my room was optimized, I committed to a consistent bedtime. I set a daily reminder on my iPhone called *Get Ready for Bed*, which went off at 10:00PM every night (i.e. nine hours before I wanted to wake up). As soon as it went off, I'd stop whatever I was doing, hit the bathroom, brush my teeth, and change out of my day clothes. I was dead serious about obeying my phone's command. Even if I was in the middle of a conversation, I'd abruptly end it so I could get ready for bed.

After I finished getting ready, I would switch my phone to Flight mode, open the Relax Melodies app, and climb in bed to read fiction for 15 minutes.[24] When I was done reading, I'd turn off the lights and focus on the rhythm of my breath until I fell asleep.

---

[24] No business or "thinking" books. Relax your mind with a story. Check out the books listed in playitaway.me/antinews

It took several nights to adjust to this change, but within a week, I was sleeping like a champion. I wasn't eating anything after 8:00PM, and I stopped drinking caffeine after 5:00PM. Those habits helped my body wind down earlier, but **the critical part was getting ready at the same time every night.** It set me in motion toward getting in bed, and ultimately re-trained my body to crave sleep at a reasonable hour.

I really can't overemphasize the importance of consistent quality sleep. Every anxious person I've met has either been in denial about how little sleep they get, or they're overlooking the fact that they're going to bed at random hours every night.

One of my readers wrote this message to me after reviewing an early draft of this chapter:

> When I began forcing myself to sleep eight hours a night, my physical health problems cleared up, my emotions balanced out, and my anxiety disappeared. My mind could function and that tight feeling around my eyes vanished. Eight hours of sleep is a miracle pill.

There was another aspect of my sleep routine that was critical for healing my anxiety: **I took a 20-minute nap every afternoon.**

Each day, immediately after I finished lunch, I would find a spot to nap – a couch, a bench, a reclined car seat, a carpeted floor, a friend's wedding...

 I'd set an alarm on my phone for 20 minutes,[25] lie on my back, close my eyes, and focus on the rhythm of my breath. I never tried to fall asleep; I just relaxed and focused on breathing in and out. Even if I didn't fall asleep (about 10% of the time), I always felt refreshed and calm when my alarm went off.

Naps are awesome. I wish I could be a salesman for naps. We all took them every day when we were kids, so... why should we stop taking them just because we're older? Take a quick nap in the afternoon, even if you have to cut your lunch break short. Then force yourself to get ready for bed at the same time every night. You'll be more relaxed and far less anxious — guaranteed.

FREQUENCY: Aim for 8 hours each night, and one 20-minute nap every afternoon.

COST: Free.

[25] Do not exceed 20 minutes for your daily nap. Otherwise you run the risk of falling into a deep sleep.

DO IT NOW: Set a daily reminder on your phone to *Get Ready for Bed,* nine hours prior to your target wake time. Set another reminder to take a nap after lunch. Plug your cell phone charger in an outlet that's far away from your bed. Cover your windows so your bedroom is as dark as possible. Drop the temperature in your bedroom to 68-70 degrees. Download the Relax Melodies app to drown out disruptive noises.

RESOURCES: **Sweet Dreams Sleep Mask (playitaway. me/sleep)** The light! It buuurns! Use this mask to block it out.

Relax Melodies (playitaway.me/relax) The most popular free sleep aid app, with more than 10 million users worldwide. My personal favorite sleep sounds are ocean waves and crickets.

Flux (playitaway.me/flux) The bright white light that you refer to as your "computer" might be disrupting your internal rhythm. Download the free Flux application to have your screen's lighting automatically switch to a sunset hue in the evening.

Philips Wake-up Light (playitaway.me/ wakeup) If you despise alarms as much as I do, then check out the Wake-up Light. It makes waking up gradual and pleasant.

BONUS POINTS

CUDDLING

Things are never quite as scary
when you've got a best friend.

— CALVIN AND HOBBES

I knew isolation and loneliness were major contributors to my anxiety.[26] I hated feeling so disconnected from other people, so I started making a real effort to NOT be alone – even when I was sleeping.

Cuddling turned out to be an extremely effective anxiety-killer. It allowed me to feel safe and comfortable while having extended physical contact with someone I cared about (which – in my humble opinion – is a vital activity that isn't encouraged enough in our culture).

My girlfriend usually slept over, but an alternative was just to curl up on the couch and embrace each other for a half hour.

---

[26] Loneliness is as strong of a predictor of early death as alcoholism or smoking a pack of cigarettes a day. It's an even stronger predictor than obesity or a sedentary lifestyle. That's why anxious people need to do whatever they can to spend more quality time with positive people (playing and cuddling are great places to start).

It wasn't always a romantic activity; it was mostly just about relaxing, feeling secure and affectionate, and synchronizing our breathing.

Humans need to touch each other in order to remain in good health. Infants who don't experience enough physical contact with their caretakers fail to develop properly. Sadly, it's very difficult for single adults to experience extended physical contact on a regular basis. That's one of the unfortunate byproducts of our isolating culture, but there are ways to remedy the problem.

If you don't have a significant other, you can either cuddle with your pet (dogs are the best) or get a massage each week. And if you're feeling brave, you can ask someone if they'd be willing to help you ax your anxiety via cuddling. I know this sounds like an awkward request, but as long as you pose the question in a non-creepy way, you can usually get someone on-board. Want to know why? Because most people are deprived of physical touch and true companionship, and they secretly crave it just as much as you do.

For those who are tapping their fingers together like a scheming Mr. Burns — Don't be a creep. Asking somebody to cuddle isn't a ruse to score at the frat house; it's a legitimate means to help you feel better. You have to be sincere while proposing this or they're going to be a little freaked out. It's not so much *what* you're proposing, it's *how* you're proposing it.

Whether your cuddling is platonic or sexual isn't really my concern, though the latter is certainly effective for reducing stress (and you get to tell your partner that you want to... wait for it... ... *Lay It Away*[27]). However, if your desire to get romantic while cuddling is going to create more anxiety, then you should either pick a different partner or just sleep solo.

And if your ideal cuddling partner turns you down, don't sweat it. Just stay focused on getting consistent quality sleep, 20-minute naps, hugging friends (i.e. standup cuddling), and the occasional massage.

FREQUENCY: As needed.

COST: For obvious reasons, you should not
                pay for this.

DO IT NOW: Invite someone over for a movie/cuddle
                night. Accept that there's no way to
                make this request sound normal and that
                it might get turned down. Try it anyway.
                Then schedule a massage.

RESOURCES: **Cuddle Party (cuddleparty.com)**
                This organization has been hosting events

---

[27] See what I did there? This book is already a franchise.

for the last 10 years all over the US, as well as Australia, Canada, England, Denmark, Sweden, and South Africa. Attendees get to relax, chat, cuddle, or just hang out. It may not be right for you, but it's an option.

OBSERVE YOUR THOUGHTS

'Stop!' I cried imploringly to my god-like mind.

— A CONFEDERACY OF DUNCES

When I first started meditating, I was constantly stressing over how bad I was at it. I couldn't resist the urge to scratch my skin. I couldn't sit in the lotus position. My shoulders would hunch. My back would get sore. But the worst part was that my mind was always wandering:

Breathe... Straight spine... Breathe... Waste of time... You're barely a minute in... Look who can count... Easy... Zen imposter... Fake Buddha... Silence... What's the ex up to... Facebook knows... It always knows!... Santa... Jesus is Santa... Buddha... Meditate... Breathe... Zen things... Ren rings... Ren and Stimpy... Stop it... Nicki Minaj... Cultural bankruptcy... You can't rhyme "Nicki" with "Nicki"... 'Starships' is catchy... I hate myself... I love myself... Millenials... Silence... Don't scratch... No touching!... Prison... Stop thinking... When did I get old... Santa Minaj... Damnit.

Then I'd give up and distract myself with the internet for the next several hours. Impressive, no?

I didn't realize it at the time, but it was *my resistance to my own thoughts* that was making meditation so difficult. The more I tried to shut my brain up, the more noise it made. The more I resisted my thoughts, the harder they fought back.

Then one day, out of sheer frustration, I gave up. I stopped wishing for my bad thoughts to go away, and just let them run wild while I sat there in silence. I was like a parent who was tired of chasing their crazy kids around, so I just gave up and calmly watched them.

Amazingly, it worked. Meditating became so much easier when I observed my thoughts like a detached outsider. Each morning, I would sit cross-legged with my back against the wall and close my eyes for 10 minutes. Then I'd just observe myself. Every thought that my mind produced – no matter how nerve-wracking or obnoxious – was allowed to make as much noise as it wanted. Instead of trying to control and change these thoughts into peaceful silence, I just watched them do their thing, like they were clouds passing by.

My thoughts weren't good or bad; they were just thoughts. I didn't need to make them perfect, or assign them any value. They all received the exact same treatment: *detached indifference.* When I got bored with them, I'd shift my focus back to the rhythm of my breathing. It was like a relaxing mental workout where there could be no failure.

After two weeks of observing my thoughts for 10 minutes each morning, my mind wasn't able to scare me. My thoughts only had power when I granted them that authority. The incessant chirping in my brain that freaked me out for months was now background noise.

Think of it this way: If you were in a room full of people who were all laughing and pointing at you, and there was no way for you to escape, how long would it take before you stopped caring? How long would it take for your panic and shame to turn into apathy and annoyance? That's how you should think about your stressful thoughts — as a room full of obnoxious people trying to wind you up. You can either let them harass you every single day, or you can practice not responding to them.

Don't resist your stressful thoughts or wish for them to change. Welcome them, observe them, and get bored with them. Calmly return to your breathing and observe that instead. If you struggle with this, try to inhale deep into your belly, then think of a single word (like Peace) as you slowly exhale.[28]

---

[28] Or you can just count; think of the next number with each exhale.

You can also lay on your back with your eyes closed while you're meditating.[29]

FREQUENCY: 10 minutes in the morning, or as needed.

COST: Free.

DO IT NOW: Sit cross-legged with your back against a wall, or lay down on your back. Set a timer on your phone for 2 minutes. Close your eyes. Practice watching your thoughts as though you're a detached observer. Alternative: Go on a 10-minute solo run and only pay attention to the rhythm of your breathing (no music allowed!)

RESOURCES: **Meditation Timer (playitaway.me/ meditate)** I use this app to transition out of mediation sessions. Instead of alarm clock noises, this app has a variety of singing bowl and chime sounds you can choose from.

Turning the Mind Into an Ally **(playitaway.me/mind)** This beginner's guide to meditation is highly recommended for those interested in Buddhism.

---

[29] I prefer to sit, as I have a tendency to fall asleep whenever I'm laying down.

***Remember Be Here Now* (playitaway. me/now)** This book's reminder to live in the present changed my life. I later discovered that *Be Here Now* inspired Steve Jobs' trip to India and his experiments with LSD.

***Search Inside Yourself* (playitaway.me/ search)** Based on the hugely popular meditation course at Google, this book shows how you can practice mindfulness in life and work.

Zazen (zazensf.com). This place was my sanctuary in San Francisco. Once a week, I'd spend an hour meditating in a soundproof, pitch-black floatation tank that was filled with warm water and Epsom salt. Sounds extreme, but floating was super relaxing and peaceful for me. Search on Yelp for "floatation tanks" near you and give it a shot. Costs about $60 per hour.

NINJA TECHNIQUE

PLAY AWAY YOUR PANIC ATTACKS

My focus is to forget the pain of life. Forget the pain, mock the pain, reduce it. And laugh.

— JIM CARREY

The thought of having a panic attack in public kept me locked up in my apartment. I envisioned myself laying on the floor of some restaurant, clutching my chest while trying to assure everyone around me that I was fine... Yikes. I wanted to prevent that scenario at all costs.

I noticed that my panic attacks were running through the same sequence each time:

(1) I'd convince myself that something really bad (and highly unlikely) was going to happen.

(2) I would obsess over all the potential ramifications of that really bad thing happening.

(3) I'd become acutely aware of my heartbeat and its rising pace.

(4) My mind began playing an ominous loop that told me I was going crazy, and that I was going to die.

(5) I would freak out, hyperventilate, and lay on the ground for 20 minutes.

It was that first step – convincing myself that something really bad was going to happen – that set the entire sequence in motion. I wondered if I could make it impossible to take myself seriously. That, I suspected, might stop the panic attack in its tracks.

The method I came up with was simple: **I would say all of my worries out loud in the most ridiculous voice I could conjure**. I wouldn't resist the thoughts or try to hide from them; I would bring them out in the open and dress them down in the voice of a chipmunk on helium. Or as the Swedish Chef from The Muppets. Or Kenny Powers. Or Arnold Schwarzenegger. Or Ron Burgundy.

As I mocked my worries in a goofy character's voice, the tension in my body loosened up. I'd snap out of my seriousness as I embellished my worries into outrageous scenarios. I threw in wild hand gestures and talked even louder. It was like I was doing improv comedy with myself.

After about 30 seconds, I was so distracted by my absurd behavior that I was no longer processing my worries. I could only focus on how ridiculous I sounded. I was like a baby whose crying switched to giggling in a matter of seconds. Better yet, I was like a funeral attendee who thought of something funny, and couldn't help but laugh.

My method was silly, juvenile, and kind of crazy, but it worked for me. It helped me loosen up and laugh at myself. My worries became impossible to take seriously and the impending panic attack faded away.

Mocking your worries might feel awkward or very difficult at first. That's okay. It takes practice before you can start having fun with yourself. But this is a great technique to experiment with because it's entirely possible to convert your worrying into something funny.

Try not to think *Why isn't this working yet?* Just let go your expectations and focus on the sound of your voice. If you start hyperventilating, go drink a full glass of water. Once you feel hydrated and your breathing has leveled out, try mocking your worries again.

FREQUENCY: As needed.

COST: Free.

DO IT NOW: Practice saying your worries out loud in the voice of a funny character. Do this for 60 seconds.

RESOURCES: **Tom Cat 2 (playitaway.me/tomcat)** Not comfortable speaking in a goofy voice? Use this app to have your worries repeated back to you by an animated cat. Surprisingly fun and effective.

Impressions by Isaac (playitaway.me/voices) If you need inspiration, watch this talented kid produce every single funny voice you can imagine.

Raptor Mascot on Rollerblades (playitaway.me/mascot) Each time I watch this video, I can't help but crack up. If all else fails, just keep watching this on repeat until you're no longer worried.

BONUS POINTS

BECOME YOUR OWN BEST FRIEND

It's impossible to heal your anxiety if you're constantly scolding yourself for not feeling normal. You need to be loving and supportive. The best way to do that is by quietly venting to yourself and practicing gratitude through writing.

Whenever you get really stressed out, grab a pen and a few pieces of paper. **Write down every single thing you're currently worrying about**. Don't filter your words or resist your feelings. Be brutally honest about what you are going through. Expose your fears and insecurities so you can see them outside of yourself.

Once you're finished, go back and read through everything you just wrote. Then take out another few sheets of paper, and write down one reason why you're grateful for every single thing you're worried about. It doesn't matter how awful or irredeemable that source of stress has been; **come up with one reason why you're thankful to have experienced it.**

This is the best method for transforming mental poison into spiritual nourishment. Writing unlocks the gates of your mental prison, which allows your brain to decompress and breathe. And practicing gratitude for each of your stressors helps you see your life in a more positive light.

I can't overstate how critical writing was for retaining my sanity. It was one of the few activities that calmed me down and made me feel better. Even when I felt like death, I was setting aside time to write down everything that was bothering me. Writing to myself (combined with meditation) helped me recognize that all of my thoughts were acceptable. That's how

I learned to be okay with myself again. It's how I became my own best friend.

I'm a major advocate for writing worries out by hand (rather than typing). It's slow and kind of painful, but there's something magical about the process. You are simultaneously venting and listening to your most private thoughts, and no one is there to interrupt or argue with you (plus, you're not being distracted by the internet). The practice is extremely therapeutic, and for me, it's a lot more emotionally powerful than typing.

Whether you keep or throw away your written thoughts is completely up to you. This is just a technique that can help you love yourself more.

FREQUENCY: As needed.

COST: Free.

DO IT NOW: Take out a few pieces of paper. Write down everything that you're stressed out about. Then come up with one reason you're grateful for those sources of stress.

RESOURCES: **Moleskine Journal (playitaway.me/ moleskine)** The most beloved brand in notebooks, sketchbooks, and journals. Great for travelers, writers, and note-takers.

END OF WEEK 2 - ASSESSMENT

- ✓ Did you have at least two sessions of guilt-free play with your friends?
- ✓ Did you get 15 minutes of sunlight and fresh air each day?
- ✓ Did you optimize your room for great sleep?
- ✓ Did you go to bed at the same time each night?
- ✓ Did you take a nap each day after lunch?
- ✓ Did you observe your thoughts for 10 minutes each morning?

ONGOING:

- ✓ Did you do the *Remove Your Anchors* exercise?
- ✓ Have your simple solutions been effective?

On a scale of 0 - 100%, how much did your anxiety drop this week?

WEEK 3 - HEAL YOUR BODY

1. *Eat Healthy Meals with Healthy Friends*
2. *Release Pent Up Frustration*
3. *T.R.E. - Trauma Releasing Exercises*

EAT HEALTHY MEALS

WITH HEALTHY

FRIENDS

Tell me what you eat, and I will tell you

what you are.

— JEAN ANTHELME BRILLAT-SAVARIN

The old saying is true: You are what you eat. And if the food you're consuming is foreign, toxic, and difficult to digest, you will feel sick, anxious, and constipated.[30] It's impossible to feel healthy if you're subsisting on foods that have zero nutritional value.

When I was at the height of my anxiety, I was regularly eating

---

[30] Sadly, most Americans subsist almost entirely on addictive foods that do not exist in nature — foods that have been chemically altered, processed, refined, and cooked in artery-clogging gunk. The human digestive system cannot process these foods without getting backed up and coated with mucus. And as a result of this Standard American Diet (and our collective lack of play), we have become the most diseased and obese population in the history of mankind... WE'RE NUMBER ONE! The irony, of course, is that when our bodies finally break down from decades of playing human garbage disposal, we end up spending all our money on medicine and surgery just so we can keep eating toxic junk for a few more years. Silly humans.

foods that I knew were toxic on a daily basis — fast food, junk food, ice cream, pizza, alcohol… But I didn't care. I was just so desperate for quick and easy forms of comfort, even though they ultimately made me feel worse. The food highs disappeared as quickly as they came, and I'd run off to find another stimulant to numb my bad feelings. Of course, I only ate like a slob when I was alone. When other people were with me, my eating habits magically cleaned themselves up.

The way I broke out of my unhealthy eating habits was by regularly eating meals with healthy friends.[31] I picked a few friends of mine who were in undeniably good health (clear glowing skin, bright eyes, high energy, toned muscles[32]), and asked if they'd be willing to sit down for a few meals together during the week. Then I copied them by eating whatever they were eating. After a few weeks of regularly dining with my healthy friends, I was feeling and looking vigorous again.

I wanted to eat with my healthy friends as often as possible, so three of my buddies and I organized a weekly dinner night.

[31] This also allowed me to spend more face-to-face time with people I liked, which is something that a lot of remote workers and freelancers tend to neglect.

[32] You might have friends who only eat low fat, low calories, or mostly vegetarian. Unfortunately, those dietary restrictions often lead to burn out and poor health. Don't adopt someone else's diet just because it *sounds* good; assess the overall health of the eater! How vigorous do they look? Is their energy naturally high? Is their demeanor lively and upbeat? Is their skin radiant?

We'd all bring a dish to share, or one person would cook a full meal for the group. We wouldn't post pictures of our food on Instagram, or update Facebook to let people know we were eating dinner together. We just focused on enjoying the food and the company.

Almost every meal consisted of three ingredients: one type of protein, one type of vegetable, and one healthy side (this formula is basically a variation of the Paleo Diet). Here are the foods I was most frequently eating:

PROTEIN

- Grass-fed beef
- Free range chicken
- Cage free pastured eggs
- Wild Alaskan salmon

VEGETABLE

- Kale
- Spinach
- Broccoli
- Zucchini
- Bell peppers
- Brussels sprouts
- Collard greens
- Bok choy

SIDE

- Avocado
- Blueberries
- Cherries
- Black Mission Figs
- Sweet potatoes
- Black beans
- Almonds
- Sauerkraut

For each meal, I consumed a good amount of protein (the portion size was roughly the size of my fist), a ton of vegetables, and a handful or two of the side. I cooked with a couple tablespoons of Kerrygold Irish Butter or coconut oil (healthy sources of fat). I never restricted myself or felt guilty for eating "too much." I always ate until I was content.

During the week, I didn't eat any bread, pasta, or dairy products. I never drank soda, fruit juice, or beverages that contained milk. Instead, I just had water, coconut water, or tea.

Of course, my diet wasn't perfect. I would break my own rules on occasion. But I wouldn't chastise myself if I had some dark chocolate or a couple glasses of wine. Nor would I feel guilty if I ate junk food on the weekend. I was just trying to get in the habit of eating with my healthy friends, and to cut most (but not all) of the toxic crap out of my diet.

My transition to a healthier diet was *gradual* and *forgiving*, rather than abrupt and perfect (which is doomed to fail). But the real key to getting my eating habits back on track was *having meals with healthy friends*. Eating is a social activity; we have a tendency to go along with whatever foods the people around us are eating. It's super difficult to have to constantly resist unhealthy foods, so try to eat with healthy people who won't force you into fighting temptation.

FREQUENCY:	Aim for at least 3 meals with healthy friends per week.
COST:	$5-100+ per meal. Depends on how many people are eating, along with the quality and quantity of the food.
DO IT NOW:	Schedule dinner with two of your healthiest friends this week.
RESOURCES:	**Slow Carb Diet (playitaway.me/ slowcarb)** Having a tough time sticking with Paleo? Check out Tim Ferriss' Slow Carb Diet, which has helped thousands of people (including both of my parents) eat healthier AND lose more than 20+ pounds of fat. Tim's diet calls for vegetables, meat, and legumes – six days a week.[33] Then there's a cheat day, where you can eat and drink anything you want for 24 hours.

BONUS POINTS

FIX MICRONUTRIENT DEFICIENCIES

For a few months, I was feeling unusually fatigued. I had

---

[33] Slow Carb doesn't allow fruit, except on cheat days. I love fruit, so I usually have some on the side at lunch.

no idea what was causing it. I was getting good sleep, I was eating healthy, and I was exercising regularly. I did some research, and found that I had a ton of symptoms for Vitamin B-12 deficiency: I felt mildly depressed, I had very little motivation, I was short of breath, my brain was foggy, and my fingers occasionally went numb.

Vitamin B-12 is in meat, fish, and certain dairy products.[34] The normal range for B-12 is between 500 and 1,000 pg/ml (picograms per milliliter), and if your levels fall below 500 pg/ml, your brain ages twice as fast. In other words, if your body isn't absorbing enough B-12, your mind rapidly deteriorates and stops functioning properly. Holy Guacamole!

When I got tested for B-12 deficiency, the results showed that my levels were **200 pg/ml** — less than half of the minimum amount my body required. Even though I was eating meat almost every single day, I was still massively deficient.

I immediately began taking Vitamin B-12 liquid drops — 1,000 mcg every day, sublingually (under the tongue). Within one week, I could already feel a difference. I was less foggy and more energetic. When I got tested again for B-12 a month later, my levels had shot up to **529 pg/ml**. I was back in the normal range.

---

[34] If you're a vegetarian or vegan, you're likely deficient in B-12.

A few of my friends took micronutrient deficiency tests, as well. None of them had B-12 levels as low as mine, but they were all deficient in something. One found he was deficient in magnesium. Another was deficient in selenium, while another was deficient in potassium. All of them took measures to correct their deficiencies, brought their levels back up to the normal ranges, and felt like new people. Their minds were clear and sharp, and their energy went through the roof.

Below is a list of three common deficiencies that *tend to amplify anxiety*. If one were so inclined, one could actively work on ingesting an ample amount of these nutrients for 30 days, while assessing their anxiety levels every week. That might prove to be a worthwhile experiment, but only if one were so inclined.[35]

1. **The Vitamin B club.** I was deficient in B-12 (methylcobalamin, found in meat), but other people might be deficient in B-2 (riboflavin, found in yogurt, spinach, almonds, and eggs), or B-5 (pantothenic acid, found in avocados, mushrooms, and sweet potatoes),

---

[35] I know I sound coy, but that's because it's important to remain skeptical of my suggestions. Just because I say something might work doesn't mean you should run out and buy a bunch of supplements. You need to do your own research first! Granted, it's very unlikely that any of these nutrients will harm you if you ingest them. Still, it's best to remain cautious about putting things into your body, especially when you know nothing about them.

or B-6 (pyridoxal phosphate, found in tuna, chicken, turkey, and cod). Fortunately, it's possible to get the recommended dose of all the B vitamins by taking a B-complex pill once per day. Check out the resources below for the brand I take.

(2) **Omega-3 Fatty Acids.** You can find omega-3 in salmon, fish oil, hemp seeds, flax seeds, and chia seeds. I take 2-4 servings of Nordic Natural's cod liver oil pills each day, which contains a solid dose of the three fatty acids: EPA, DHA, and ALA.

(3) **Potassium.** Easy deficiency to develop, but just as easy to fix. Good sources of potassium include sweet potatoes, bananas, oranges, tomatoes, potatoes, and beets.

Everyone should get tested for micronutrient deficiencies at some point. There are plenty of reasons why this is a smart move, but for me, the most obvious reason is because of *our soil*. The most nutritious foods we eat absorb their nutrients from the soil they grow in, and the purity of our soil has been severely compromised through hyper-aggressive agriculture and mining practices. So even if you are eating a natural and well-balanced diet, you could still be lacking in some of the key nutrients your brain and body need in order to function properly.

One final note on deficiencies: It's possible that your gut isn't absorbing nutrients properly. If you suspect that's the case, you might consider taking a probiotic supplement to introduce more healthy bacteria into your stomach. You can also get more healthy bacteria by eating fermented foods, like sauerkraut and kimchi.

FREQUENCY:
Once you've been tested for deficiencies, ingest an ample amount of the desired nutrients (via food or supplements) for 30 days. Get tested again and re-assess.

COST:
Varies, depending on whether you're ingesting food or supplements. $80 for the B-12 deficiency test at Any Lab Test Now. $400 for the micronutrient test. I know, I know - it's expensive.

DO IT NOW:
Research the nutrients in this chapter to see if there's anything you might be deficient in. Visit anylabtestnow.com to find a location nearby. Schedule an appointment to get a micronutrient test.

RESOURCES:
[None of these resources are affiliate links. I will not earn money if you decide to purchase anything I suggest.]

Any Lab Test Now (anylabtestnow.com)
You can get tested for deficiencies in just a few minutes at Any Lab Test Now and have the results emailed to you within 48 hours. You can also get micronutrient tests at your doctor's office, but (depending on which state you're in) they will probably make you jump through a few hoops first.

Vitamin B-Complex Caps by TwinLab (playitaway.me/vitaminb) This covers all of your bases for the B vitamins. These pills are free from common allergens, like soy, yeast, barley, wheat, and lactose.

Nordic Natural's Arctic Cod Liver Oil (playitaway.me/fishoil) I take 2-4 servings of these pills per day.

RELEASE PENT UP FRUSTRATION

The doctor gave me a relaxation cassette. When my
blood pressure gets too high, the man on the tape
tells me to say 'SERENITY NOW!'

Are you supposed to yell it?

The man on the tape wasn't specific.

— Seinfeld

My anxiety changed my behavior. I usually joked around with people, but suddenly, I was walking on eggshells in every interaction. I was submissive, agreeable, and excessively nice. I didn't realize it until a couple friends told me I had to stop worrying about hurting their feelings.[36]

This new behavior was partially caused by how isolated and lonely I felt (I couldn't stand the thought of my friends shunning me), but mostly, it stemmed from a fear of confrontation. I was trying to avoid an emotional breakdown because I knew if someone screamed in my face or tried to

---

[36] I remember a friend offering me a snack, then making a joke about how I never shared. I was so paranoid that he was accusing me of being a bad person that I apologized profusely while he stood there looking confused.

fight me, I'd probably fall apart on the spot.

I masked how I felt for months, always trying to maintain poise. Even when I was out with a group of friends, I just faked my enthusiasm by mimicking theirs, doing my best to hide my frustration.[37] I didn't talk to anyone about how I felt because, for better or worse, guys don't really talk about feelings.

When guys hang out, we joke around and mess with each other. Our interactions are light and fun, and excessive displays of emotion (especially fear or sadness) are viewed as weak and emasculating. We usually don't discuss feelings because it's always been off-limits, so it makes us really uncomfortable. Almost every man has been raised to value how he *thinks* more than how he *feels*, and because a lot of our feelings aren't easy to rationalize, we block ourselves from expressing them.

While I was putting a clamp on the feelings I didn't want to show, I was unknowingly screwing up all the others. Every emotion I experienced felt clumsy and filtered. My face started twitching as my body begged me to release the frustration that

---

[37] I distinctly remember being in a bar one night, looking around the room and feeling so depressed that I was participating in the weekly ritual of poisoning myself with alcohol, just so I could have superficial interactions with people I'd probably never see again. And it was my fault. My priorities were screwed up. I was working all the time, and never having guilt-free play with my friends.

was bubbling over.

One night, I received a phone call that sent me over the edge. I don't even remember what the call was about. All I know is that right after I hung up, I went into my bedroom, shut the door, wailed on my mattress until I collapsed, then wept for 10 minutes. I slept like a rock that night, and felt like a new person the following morning.

The next day, I sat down with a friend I was really upset with. I'd been holding in my frustration with them for so long, simply to avoid getting into an argument. I talked to them face-to-face and admitted that I'd been angry but reluctant to speak up. I didn't verbally attack them; I just asked them to hear me out, explained how I felt and why I was upset, then asked how we could fix the situation.[38]

I repeated this process with a few more people that I was frustrated with. We didn't always resolve our issues, but having a levelheaded conversation, where we both tried to empathize and understand each other, released a lot of the tension we both felt. And usually, we bonded and grew closer just by talking.

It was really hard to initiate those uncomfortable discussions, but it was completely worthwhile. It helped me realize that I

[38] If you're not sure how to approach someone like this, check out the book *Difficult Conversations* by Douglas Stone.

was doing things that were upsetting those people too, which I needed to fix in order to make things right. Those realizations saved some of my most important relationships from falling apart.[39]

You can't be happy and awesome and stoic all of the time. Period. It's just simply not possible. Life is not always great; sometimes it's really tough. That's why you were equipped with a full spectrum of emotions; they help you get through the hard times. Stop resisting the expression of your being and listen to your body. Screw perfection, screw poise – just let go. If you're sad, give yourself permission to bawl. If you're angry, go beat something to a pulp (preferably a pillow or cushion), then yell at the top of your lungs. Keep doing it until you're exhausted.

When you're relaxed and composed, go speak with the people who have been upsetting you. Be honest and vulnerable, hear each other out, and keep talking until you find a solution both sides are happy with.

Feel better? I thought so.[40]

---

[39] Some people are impossible to talk with directly. They might be emotionally abusive, or maybe they just never listen to you. If that's the case, you might want to consider talking to a therapist instead

[40] If you're feeling suicidal and can't express how you feel to the people around you, dial 1-800-273-TALK. Calls are free and confidential, and the line is open 24-hours a day.

FREQUENCY: As needed. This isn't a one-time technique that will cure you; you'll need to practice expressing your emotions on an ongoing basis (even when you're not watching sports).

COST: Free, or extremely expensive if you like to destroy property.

DO IT NOW: What are you feeling? Go into your bedroom, close the door, and express it. Who are you upset with? Go have an honest discussion with them face-to-face.

RESOURCES: **Stress-releasing exercise.** You can go to the batting cages, take boxing classes, do yoga... Any physical activity that allows you to release your emotional tension.

Difficult Conversations: How to Discuss What Matters Most **(playitaway.me/ difficult)** If the thought of being mildly confrontational toward another person sends you into a panic, you ought to read this book.

T.R.E. - TRAUMA RELEASING EXERCISES

Note from Charlie: This next technique is going to sound bizarre. I don't blame you if you're skeptical, but it worked really well for me and there's a good amount of research to back up the benefits of T.R.E.

One of the weirdest effects of anxiety is how much tension builds up in your body. I couldn't even take a deep breath because my stomach always trembled, like it was being stretched to its limits. Relaxing felt physically impossible.

My body was so tense because I was constantly in fight-or-flight mode. Every day, I was producing the energy needed to survive a life-threatening event. The problem was that this event was *in my mind*; it was imaginary and it never took place. I had all this excess energy that wasn't being released, so I became extremely high-strung.

A friend recommended that I check out T.R.E. (Trauma Releasing Exercises), which helped him conquer his anxiety. I watched a few videos of T.R.E. on YouTube and immediately thought it was fake. The clips showed people lying on the ground as their bodies went into spastic tremors. Their movements looked comical and freaky, like they were in the middle of an exorcism.

I learned that tremors are a natural means for mammals to discharge excess energy after a traumatic event. The tremors release our body's surplus of adrenaline after it's no longer needed for survival. I watched footage of antelopes, bears, and other animals that had narrowly escaped an attack. Their bodies instinctively trembled for a few minutes, and then they'd act calm and normal again.[41] It was fascinating.

Unlike most species, adult humans typically prevent themselves from having tremors. Why? Because we avoid behavior that makes us look weak or vulnerable. In other words, we are so self-conscious that we unknowingly block our body's natural (yet embarrassing) function during times of great stress. As a result, we make it very difficult to overcome trauma because we're constantly holding in so much excess energy. Thankfully, T.R.E. can help.

T.R.E. was originally designed as a safe and easy way to induce tremors. Anyone who has gone through extreme trauma, from the emotionally abused to war veterans, can use these exercises to their benefit. The exercises take about 20 minutes to complete, and they're intended to induce tremors

[41] If you've ever seen a little dog shivering from the sound of loud fireworks, then you know what tremors look like.

by exhausting your leg muscles.

I bought the official T.R.E. book on my Kindle (see the resources for the link[42]), and went through all the exercises. After I completed the full circuit, I lied on the ground and was STUNNED as my back, hips, and legs shook rapidly in sporadic bursts for 20 minutes. The tremors weren't painful at all; the sensation actually felt relaxing and natural. I was just astounded by how vigorously my body shook. I looked like a vibrating cell phone. After my body's tremors finally subsided, I went to lie down on my bed and immediately fell into a deep sleep.

I performed these exercises three nights per week, for three weeks. They were hugely effective for releasing the physical tension my body was holding in. I can't show or describe all of the exercises here, as I don't want to take credit for a routine I didn't create. But if you're interested in giving T.R.E. a shot, you should check out the book in the resources below.

I know T.R.E. might sound kooky, or even a little scary. But it's really not bad at all. It's basically just a series of stretches that help your body thaw itself out by alleviating your chronic tension. Your tremors will definitely make your body move

[42] I have no affiliation with T.R.E. or David Berceli (the doctor who came up with it). I'm just a fan because the technique worked well for me.

in strange ways though, so be sure to do these exercises in a relaxed environment where you won't feel self-conscious.

FREQUENCY:	Every other day for three weeks. Then as needed.
COST:	$10 for the book.
DO IT NOW:	Visit traumarelease.co.nz and watch the 8-minute Tremors video to see how it works.
RESOURCES:	**Trauma Releasing Exercises (playitaway.me/tre)** This short book explains the trauma recovery process in uncomplicated language. The last chapter includes photos and descriptions of the exercises, which elicit tremors that release deep chronic tension in the body.

BONUS POINTS

5-MINUTE COLD SHOWERS

I hope you're ready for another crazy suggestion, because I know for a fact most people will read this section and immediately say, *"I would never do that!"* It's up to you, of course, but this tip is definitely worth trying out.

I first discovered the benefits of cold showers while I was working on *The 4-Hour Body*. In the book, there's a chapter called "Ice Age" which features the story of Ray Cronise, a material scientist at NASA who tripled his fat loss through intermittent cold exposure. Ray did things like drink a gallon of ice water each morning, take ice baths, and go on "shiver walks" in the winter without a jacket.

Increasing fat loss wasn't particularly interesting to me, but I was fascinated by the effects that cold exposure could have on a person's well being. For instance, I discovered that being in cold water for extended periods was a natural remedy for warding off depression and improving the body's immune system.

During the month I healed my anxiety, I started taking 5-minute ice cold showers every morning. I always felt great afterwards, and my anxious energy was tempered for at least an hour.

My routine was simple. I'd start with 30 seconds of warm water, and then I'd turn the faucet all the way down to the coldest temperature. Then I wove a tapestry of obscenities for 100 seconds as the freezing water pounded on my back. Then I rotated clockwise, lifted up my arm so the water could hit my left side, and counted to 50. I rotated two more times so the cold water could douse my front (100 seconds) and right side (50 seconds). After the five minutes was up, I felt *extremely* awake and energized.[43]

FREQUENCY: Every day for ongoing benefits, such as reduced depression and increased energy.

COST: Free.

DO IT NOW: Hop in the shower. Twist the faucet to the coldest setting for 30 seconds. Feel the shock, swear profusely, and survive.

RESOURCES: **The 4-Hour Body (playitaway.me/4hb)**
If you want to read the full explanation on how extremely cold temperatures can be good for you (along with many other cool health-related tidbits), check out *The 4HB*. It's one of the most highlighted books of all-time, according to Amazon.

---

[43] Some people report that cold water has a tranquilizing effect. This has never been the case for me, but you may want to try your first cold shower on the weekend so you're not falling asleep at work.

END OF WEEK 3 - ASSESSMENT

✓ Did you schedule meals with your healthiest friends this week?

✓ Did you physically express any frustration you've been feeling?

✓ Did you initiate an open discussion with anyone you've been avoiding?

✓ Did you try the Trauma Releasing Exercises?

✓ Did you try taking a cold shower?

ONGOING

✓ *Remove Your Anchors*?

✓ Guilt-free play with friends?

✓ Bed at the same time?

✓ Nap after lunch?

✓ Observing thoughts in the morning?

On a scale of 0 - 100%, how much did your anxiety drop this week?

WEEK 4 - HEAL YOUR WORLD

1. *Live in a Happier Environment*
2. *Take an Unplugged Nature Vacation*
3. *Intentional Acts of Kindness*

LIVE IN A HAPPIER ENVIRONMENT

Living in downtown San Francisco was a major drag on my energy. For my friends, it was a vibrant city with an innovative culture. For me, it was crowded, dirty, and noisy. My friends saw entrepreneurs and artists. I saw workaholics, homeless people, and traffic.

My environment wore me out, so each weekend, I drove across the Golden Gate Bridge for a hike in the hills or to hang out on a secluded beach. That helped a lot, but it still wasn't enough. I wanted to move out for good. The problem was: I felt trapped by all the stuff I'd accumulated. The things I owned were preventing me from packing my bags and moving out.

I decided to get rid of any possession I hadn't used in the last 30 days. I spent a weekend listing items on eBay and Craigslist, and donating stuff to the GoodWill. I didn't care if I only made back 10% on what I originally paid; the physical and mental space I regained was worth far more than the financial hit.

After I got rid of the majority of my possessions, I told my roommates I was moving, and sold my remaining furniture to the person who took my spot. When I arrived in a remote mountain town in Colorado (where I lived for the next several months), I immediately felt better. Things were quieter, calmer, and cleaner. I could breathe easy and relax. I felt sane again.

Whether you're consciously aware of it or not, you are affected by everything surrounding you – your possessions, your room, your home, your friends, your neighborhood, and your city. If your surroundings aren't conducive to your health and happiness, you will feel exhausted all the time. But if your environment is completely aligned with the life you desire, you'll feel rejuvenated. You'll come alive.

The first step is to pay attention to how you feel in the rooms you spend the most time in – your bedroom, your living room, your kitchen, and your office. Eliminate any possessions in those rooms that make you feel annoyed or overwhelmed or tired. Just get rid of them.[44] Adjust the lighting, coloring, plants, artwork, and furniture until you have an arrangement that makes you feel light and happy. Keep those rooms clean. Open your doors and windows to get

---

[44] Material possessions and money are replaceable. Removing physical clutter, however, is priceless. Instead of buying and owning better possessions, try to invest more of your money on fun experiences with friends (such as a road trip, a team sport, or a group dinner). Experiences are what create your fondest memories, enrich your life, and bring you closer to the people you love.

the air flowing. Only allow people you genuinely like inside. Kick anyone who drains your energy out.

The next step is to pay attention to how you feel when you're in different environments – the city, the desert, the plains, the mountains, and the ocean. Where have you felt your best? Where do you come alive? Try to spend more of your time there. If you always feel your best in a certain environment, consider moving there with friends.

FREQUENCY:	As needed.
COST:	Free to very expensive, depending on the cost of living and how drastically you change your environment.
DO IT NOW:	Make your bed. Clean your room. Donate, sell, or throw away something you haven't used in the last 30 days. Schedule a day trip with a friend to your favorite environment this weekend. If you're thinking about moving, rent an apartment in your dream location for one week (use AirBNB.com).
RESOURCES:	**Numbeo (numbeo.com)** Free tool for comparing the cost and quality of living in cities around the world.
	TaskRabbit (taskrabbit.com) Want to hire

a monthly cleaner? Need some assistance moving out? How about a feng shui expert? Whatever you need help with for improving your environment, you can find a temp worker on TaskRabbit to help solve your problem.

TAKE AN UNPLUGGED NATURE VACATION

People in the city are goin' insane.

— STEVE MILLER BAND

Whenever I'm feeling burned out, I force myself to take an unplugged nature vacation. **I relocate to a scenic environment where the skyline isn't cluttered with buildings or human activity, then I disconnect from every device with a screen.** No phone, no television, no computer. That means no texting, no calling, no email, no Facebook, no Instagram, and no *Seinfeld*. Only nature, face-to-face interactions, and books are allowed.

Unplugged nature vacations are incredibly refreshing. My mind always feels like a stuffy room that gets a sudden rush of fresh air. Instead of feeling tired all day long from a steady diet of internet content, I'm rejuvenated by real life again.

Unplugged nature vacations don't require you to buy camping equipment, to travel out of state, or to pack overnight bags. All you need to do is eliminate screens and surround yourself with Mother Nature for an extended period of time (ideally

longer than 24 hours[45]). You can take a vacation by yourself, or you can go with your friends. The point is just to disconnect and be in nature.

Give yourself permission to stop working and unplug. Don't feel guilty for taking time off. This isn't an escape from the real world – it's a chance to reconnect with it. Taking a break from modern living is the perfect opportunity to turn inward, breathe, and relax in quiet stillness.

We all need to get back in nature from time-to-time. It's our much-needed reminder that the universe is blissfully unaware of our little careers.

FREQUENCY: One weekend per month, or as needed.

COST: Between free and expensive, depending on your destination and accommodations

DO IT NOW: Go on a two-hour hike at a local park. Leave your cell phone at home. Schedule a nature vacation.

[45] Anyone can go 24 hours without using their phone or computer. There aren't any pressing matters you're going to miss, and you're definitely not as important as you think. Disconnect. Life goes on.

RESOURCES:

AirBNB (airbnb.com) The perfect service for finding short-term lodging. The site has more than 500,000 listings in 33,000 cities, in nearly every country on the planet. Listings include private rooms, apartments, castles, boats, manors, tree houses, tipis, igloos, and private islands.

Camp Grounded (campgrounded.org) Weekend summer camp for adults. Trade in your computer and cell phone for a weekend of pure unadulterated fun. Activities include hiking, stargazing, swimming in the river, capture the flag, kickball, talent show, toasting marshmallows, and more.

Escape 101 **(playitaway.me/escape)** If you want a longer break from work, this book will show you how to successfully take a sabbatical without losing all your money (or your mind).

Into the Wild **(playitaway.me/wild)** Wonderful film about the life of Christopher McCandless, who decided to leave the American Dream behind and vagabond his way to Alaska.

INTENTIONAL ACTS OF KINDNESS

There is no need for temples, no need for compli-cated philosophies. My brain and my heart are my temples; my philosophy is kindness.

— DALAI LAMA

My friend Jeff Waldman was always creating street art for our neighborhood. He hung up swings on trees in the park, made Take-a-Book-Leave-a-Book stations out of old newsstands, and handed out pre-stamped Mother's Day cards to his neighbors.

The purpose of Jeff's projects was to elicit joy from the people passing by. City officials removed a lot of his work, but it was always cool to watch him make our neighbors a little happier.

Intentional Acts of Kindness are really fun. They shut your worries up and get you out of your head for a while. They're also a great way to interact with people, make new friends, and spread good karma.

If you're not sure where to start, here are some ideas for Intentional Acts of Kindness that you can do right now:

✓ **Say "Hi."** Lock eyes with a passing stranger, smile (very important), and say hello. Keep doing this over and over.

✓ **Call an old friend.** Say that a fun memory of the two of you popped into your head, and you wanted to see how they were doing.

✓ **Facebook toasts.** Instead of using Facebook to convince people how great your life is, post something nice about one of your friends instead. Write about why you're grateful to know them.

✓ **Apologize to someone you've wronged.** No matter how nice you think you are, there's someone out there who believes you're a total jerk. Get in touch, say that what you did has been weighing on your conscience, and tell them you're sorry.

✓ **Thank someone who is rarely thanked.** Leave your trash man a Thank You note. Write a compliment about your server on the receipt. Offer your bus driver a free cup of coffee.

✓ **Mail a handwritten letter.** My mom wrote one letter each day for 30 days, letting her closest friends know why she was grateful to have them in her life. And every day that month, she got phone calls from the recipients who wanted to express their gratitude for the note.

✓ **Free hugs.** Run up to a friend and lean into it.

✓ **Free art.** Spend a day creating art and giving it away. If you're in Central Park, you might see the Roving Typist, who will write a unique short story for you, free of charge.

✓ **Volunteer to help kids with reading.** You want the next generation to be intelligent? Well, this is the most fun and effective way to ensure that happens.

✓ **Host a Couchsurfer.** Share your home with people traveling through your neighborhood. Be generous. It will make an impact on how they view the world.

✓ **Be kind to another species.** Humans are a bit

monstrous to non-humans. We cage, torture, kill, and sell practically everything that isn't us Pretty strange, considering we were all blessed with the exact same gift of existing on this planet together. Be kind, be their companions, and just let them be.

✓ **Play.** Ask your neighbors to join you.

You can never run out of love to give; it's the ultimate form of renewable energy. And if you keep generously spreading love to those around you, you won't have to worry so much about getting it in return. Somehow, it always finds its way back.

FREQUENCY:	As needed.
COST:	Free or cheap.
DO IT NOW:	Call someone you care about. Do a Facebook toast.
RESOURCES:	**Couchsurfing (couchsurfing.org)** Connect with travelers all around the world. Share your home, or find local hosts

to stay with in more than 100,000 cities.

Suicide Watch (reddit.com/r/SuicideWatch)
The people in this forum are really struggling. If you want to help save someone's life, this is where you can do it. You *can* make a difference.

***Exit Through the Gift Shop* (playitaway. me/banksy)** Fantastic and hilarious documentary about the wild world of street art. One of my all-time favorite films.

END OF WEEK 4 - ASSESSMENT

- ✓ Did you rearrange and clean your rooms so you can feel light and happy?
- ✓ Did you take a nature hike?
- ✓ Did you disconnect from screens for 24 hours this week?
- ✓ Did you commit any intentional acts of kindness?

ONGOING:

- ✓ Remove Your Anchors?
- ✓ Eating meals with healthiest friends?
- ✓ Guilt-free play with friends?
- ✓ Bed at the same time? Nap after lunch?
- ✓ Observing thoughts in the morning?

On a scale of 0 - 100%, how much did your anxiety drop this week?

OVERALL ASSESSMENT

On a scale of 0-100%, how much has your anxiety dropped since you started the 4-week plan?

FOR ONGOING HEALTH AND HAPPINESS, CONTINUE PRACTICING THE FOLLOWING TECHNIQUES...

✓ **Mind.** Remove your anchors. Enjoy guilt-free play with friends. Go to bed at the same time. Take a nap after lunch. Observe your thoughts. Practice gratitude.

✓ **Body.** Eat healthy meals with healthy friends. Get fresh air and sunshine every day. Release pent-up frustration.

✓ **World.** Create the environment you want to live in. Take nature vacations. Disconnect from screens. Commit intentional acts of kindness.

6

HOW I PLAY TODAY

I looked like I'd just climbed out of a pool. A passerby stopped to ask if I knew how much I was sweating. *Yes,* I said laughing, *it's been this way the entire time and I haven't died yet.* It was the humidity. It never let up.

I looked up at the departure screen. In three hours, I'd be back in Krabi - the city I'd left earlier that day. I'd been traveling around Thailand for a month and I wanted to extend my trip. But American tourists were only allowed to stay for 30 days at a time. That's why I flew into Malaysia, the country with the closest international airport. And because I'd left Thailand (albeit for two hours), I was now free to return for another month. Silly passport laws.

I knew nothing about Kuala Lumpur (the city I was in), but at the last minute, I decided to stay for a few days. Why not? I pulled out my phone, booked a room on HostelWorld, and then hopped on a bus headed for downtown.

I grabbed an open seat and looked around. Everyone was silently staring down at their cell phones. Two guys sat down next to me and we struck up a conversation. They were cricketers from Pakistan. It was their first visit to Malaysia, as well.

When I arrived at my hostel two hours later, I was greeted at the gate by Sza Sza - the owner's 4-year old daughter - who was holding a red balloon. She looked down at my bags, looked back up at me, and asked if we could play catch.

I was tired, sore, and dirty. My workaholic self would have politely turned this kid down, headed straight for my air-conditioned room, and laid in bed staring at my phone. But I didn't do those things. I was relaxed and well-practiced at play. I remembered what it was like.

I dropped my bags and jumped straight into a series of games. We played for three hours. I wasn't trying to prove a point or make a show of myself. It was just the thing to do. Sza Sza and I trapped monsters in the refrigerator, sailed the ocean, and played catch with her red balloon.

The next morning, the Pakistani cricketers I met on the bus came by my hostel. They invited me to join them and a few of their teammates for a trip to the water park. My workaholic self would have politely turned them down, taken my laptop to a café, and messed around on the internet. But I didn't do those things. I jumped in the taxi with the group and we headed out.

We had a blast the entire day. We whooped and hollered as we rode down the slides, and cracked up whenever we got drenched. We made jokes about our cultures, played games together, and became friends.

I didn't feel guilty for not working. I didn't chide myself for not being productive. I didn't even really process what I was doing. I was just in the moment, living again.

I returned to the hostel that evening, where I found Sza Sza on the porch with her red balloon. She laughed as I lifted her onto my shoulders. We battled the monsters then threw a party in the jungle. When we asked the other hostel guests if they wanted to join, they politely turned us down and stared back at the soft glow of their phones.

On my final day in the hostel, Sza Sza waved to me from behind the gate as I walked down the street. As I turned the corner, I could still hear her crying out, "Bye, Charlie! Bye, big brother!"

I couldn't see it for a long time, but I was the creator of my own anxious reality. I worked myself to exhaustion. I never slept. I didn't allow myself to have fun. I consumed fear-mongering news that convinced me the end was near. People absorbed and reflected my nervousness back at me, and my anxiety perpetuated itself.

When I started viewing life through the lens of *Play*, my world changed. I got rid of all the things that made me unhappy. I went outside and had guilt-free fun with my friends. All of my interactions became a dance. My inner joy shined through the smile on my face, and people reflected my playful energy right back at me. I kept this up for weeks, and then one day, I noticed... *I was surrounded by fun-loving people, all the time.* My life became great again because I chose to play.

It took me two months in Asia to realize: I don't need to be on vacation in order to play. I don't even need to stop working. I can always do it. *Play is a state of mind.*

Now, my life is a series of opportunities to have fun. The world is a playground. The people around me are playmates. And most importantly, my work is a game. Instead of killing myself for future success, I work to feel alive right now.

Of course, my life isn't perfect. Bad things still happen, and I forget from time-to-time. But when I return to the things that make me truly happy — catch, making people laugh, creating art, playing with friends — my inner tension melts away. I'm no longer serious or worried. I don't need alcohol or drugs to face the world. I can just be, and life is good.

When I think back on how much pain I used to hold in, I have to laugh. I spent all that time living in fear, when all I had to do was play it away.

(7)

HOW TO CHANGE THE WORLD

Every now and then, you'll sense a looming darkness, as though something bad is about to happen. You might see it on your TV, or in the news, or in the panicked look on your friend's face. The end is near, they'll say, and it will be every man for himself.

This is the frightened narrative of the lonely individuals who have been chronically deprived of play. Their minds are clouded with fear, and they are on an endless hunt for potential threats to their survival.

You might not see it, but these people are very sad inside. They have tricked themselves into believing their world is a frightening prison. They've fallen out of touch with their friends, so they combat their isolation the only way they know how: *by bringing others into their fear.* And as that fear spreads, they all forget how to bond, and share, and laugh, and love. They forget that life is a ride.

Fortunately, you don't have to believe these people. In fact, you can help them. And you know exactly how to do it.

If you're ready to play, put down this book, pick up your phone, and reach out to someone you care about. Say this:

> Life has been feeling too serious lately. I want to take a break and do something fun. Want to play?

Then get outside and play. Whether it's catch, or a pickup game, or just a long walk… go do something fun right now that will bring you together with the people you love. And when you're finished, tell them to play it forward by asking their friends to do the same.

You don't need more free time. You don't need more money. You can change the world when you change how you see it. It's only a choice.

Play is a state of mind – **it's a way to approach the world. Whether your world is a frightening prison or a loving playground is entirely up to you.**

WILL YOU DO ME A SOLID?

If you enjoyed *Play It Away*, would you mind taking a minute to write a review on Amazon? Even a short review helps, and it'd mean a lot to me.

If someone you care about is struggling with anxiety or workaholism, please send him or her a copy of this book. Whether you gift it to them on Amazon or email a copy of the PDF makes no difference to me.

If you'd like to order copies of this book for your company, school, or group of friends, please go to playitaway.me/order.

Finally, if you'd like to get free bonus materials from this book and receive updates on my future projects, you can sign up for my newsletter at CharlieHoehn.com. You can also follow me on Twitter @charliehoehn.

Life awaits. Go play!

THANK YOU

To all the good people who helped me stay sane...

Jeff Waldman, Molly Fiffer, Jason Hemmerle, Debbie Phillips — Thanks for being such good friends during my year of quiet crazy. Teddy Mekuria, Nick Carrel, Chris Wesley — Thanks for not letting me take my seriousness too seriously. Chad Mureta, Jason Adams — Thanks for reminding me how important it is to play at work. Laura Garner — Thanks for being a great friend when I wasn't. Luby's Concepción — Thanks for being such a loving escape. Emily Pfau — Thank you for putting up with all of my nonsense.

Tucker Max — I can't express how grateful I am for your constant

support, wisdom, and generosity.
In spite of the title you're famous
for, I've only known you as one of
my most encouraging, loyal, and
helpful friends. Thanks for being
you, and remember: You can take
My free rent, but you'll never
take MY FREE WORK!

Tim Ferriss - I was extremely
lucky to have the good fortune
of working with one of my heroes.
You presented me with more
incredible opportunities than I
knew what to do with, all while
shaping me into the person I
wanted to be. I can never fully
repay you for all you did for me;
I just hope to do you proud by
paying it forward. For your
guidance, your books, and most
of all, for showing us what was
possible... Thanks, Meng.

Ramit Sethi - Thank you for taking a shot on that eager kid who wanted to work on something fun. Your early support catapulted me into the exact position I hoped to be in, and I wouldn't have ended up here without your help. As much as I've enjoyed having you as a colleague, you've also been a great and hilarious friend. I will pay you back for the dating ad. I don't forget.

Seth Godin - Thank you for the inspiration you've provided on a daily basis for all these years. You showed me the importance whoops of doing work that matters, and not settling for a job just to pay the bills. This path is not without its challenges, but - as you said - it's worth it.

Erin Tyler, Ryan Holiday, Nils Parker, Tim Stiefler, Ann Maynard – The depth of your guys' ~~talents~~ continues to blow my mind. I'm incredibly lucky to know you all as my good friends, colleagues, and role models. Thank you for offering your insight and expertise, which made this book so much better.

Divya Pahwa, Mohnish Soundararajan, Andrew Edstrom, Edward Druce, Matt Trinetti – Thank you all for enthusiastically executing my random ideas. You guys made a great team and have bright futures ahead of you.

My amazing ~~Beta~~ Readers! Alex McCafferty, Ali Roberts, Austin Granzow, Ben Boomer, Brad Hart, Carolynn Ananian, Chee Xiong, Chris Clark, Corey Wadden, Curtis Loukes, David Isaacson,

Eric Gardner, Ian Borders, Ivana Sendecka, Janet Chang, Jessica Campbell, Justin Mares, Kate Little, Lindsay Holden, Marcie Barnes, Mary Katherine Sullivan, Matt Kress, Megan Snedden, Michael Gebben, Nick Altman, Robert Knutsson, Sachit Gupta, Scott Hughes, Therese Schwenkler, Tina Khera, Tina Shah, Yael Grover, Zach Obront (I hope that's everyone) — Thank you all for reviewing the ugly first draft of this book. Your feedback made Play It Away into something special that I hope you're proud to have been a part of. You rule!

Kinsellas, Pollocks, Cases — You tolerated two decades of tennis balls, pranks, and relentless juvenile behavior that would have driven most reasonable

people to a new neighborhood.
I'll always consider you guys
family. Thank you for never
calling the cops.

Devin, Kelly, Michelle, Ryan, Carie,
Wade, Steve, Joey, Justin, Austin,
Jake, Tony, Kevin, Zach, Dave,
Lance, Darrell, Pat, August, Em,
Linds, Jenny, Katherine, Chrissy,
Steph — No matter how much time
passes between our encounters,
we never skip a beat. We've been
playmates for more than a
decade, and I hope it remains
that way for life.

Katie — You've been my primary
prank target your entire life.
Nothing has delighted me more
than having a sister with a
deathly fear of moths. Thank you
for your dramatic reactions to
everything. (By the way, you were
adopted, sorry)

Mom, Dad – You loved and supported me for the past 27 years of hair-graying decisions. Thank you for encouraging me to have fun, for raising us in such a playful environment, and for laughing off all the times I got in trouble (e.g. injuries, suspensions, MIPs, mild vandalism, getting condiments and holidays banned, etc.) I only hope that all of my future successes result in me calling out, "What did I do?!"

To the rest of my family and friends who I've neglected to mention here – Thank you all for being so much fun. How lucky I've been to have such quality people surrounding me my entire life. I wish we could all live together and play whenever we wanted.

Last but not least, to my readers —
It still amazes me that there are
people I've never met who have
been rooting for me for years.
From the bottom of my heart,
thank you for letting me in.

Now, let's sing and dance while
the music is being played.

Enjoy your ride,

Martin Hecht

PHOTO CREDITS

Thanks so much to all the people who took such sweet, sweet pics:

Page 16 © Marcie Barnes

Page 28 © Angélica Torres

Page 31 © Judy Hoehn

Page 33 © Erin Tyler

Page 54 © Lubys Concepción

Page 71 © Molly Fiffer

Page 89 © Zach Roach

Page 138 © Jeff Waldman

Page 165 © Ryan Case

ABOUT THE AUTHOR

Charlie Hoehn is an author, marketing strategist, speaker, and play enthusiast. After graduating from Colorado State University in 2008, he studied under and worked with a number of bestselling authors, such as Ramit Sethi, Seth Godin, and Tucker Max. He worked alongside Tim Ferriss during the production and launch of *The 4-Hour Body*, which hit #1 on the New York Times bestseller list and sold over a million copies.

Charlie is the author of *Recession-Proof Graduate: How To Land The Job You Want By Doing Free Work*, a popular career guide that's been read more than 150,000 times. His work has been featured by The New York Times, NPR, CBS, TEDx, and Business Insider.

He is currently playing in Austin, Texas.

Manufactured in the United States of America
10 9 8 7 6 5 4 3 2 1

Library of Congress Cataloging-in-Publication Data
ISBN 978-0-615-91817-4

Cover Design by ErinTylerDesign.com
Cover Photo by Ryan Case

11349166R00102

Made in the USA
San Bernardino, CA
13 May 2014